Transparency and Journalism

This book offers a comprehensive, authoritative, and accessible introduction to journalistic transparency.

Pulling from historical and theoretical perspectives, *Transparency and Journalism* explains the concept of transparency and its place in journalistic practice, offering a critical assessment of what transparency can and cannot offer to journalism. The author also reviews the key theoretical claims underlying transparency and how they have been researched in different parts of the world, ultimately proposing a communication model that can be used to study the concept of transparency across journalism research. Other topics discussed include the use of algorithmic forms of transparency, the limitations of the transparency myth, and suggestions for future avenues for research.

Transparency and Journalism is an important resource for students and scholars in the field of journalism and media studies, as well as for journalists and researchers interested in delving into an ever-relevant topic for the field.

Michael Karlsson is professor in media and communication at Karlstad University, Sweden. His research interest lies primarily within digital journalism and his work has been widely published in journals such as *Digital Journalism, Journalism Studies, Journalism, Journalism and Mass Communication Quarterly, Journal of Computer-Mediated Communication*, and *Communication Theory*.

T0347590

Disruptions: Studies in Digital Journalism
Series editor: Bob Franklin

Disruptions refers to the radical changes provoked by the affordances of digital technologies that occur at a pace and on a scale that disrupts settled understandings and traditional ways of creating value, interacting and communicating both socially and professionally. The consequences for digital journalism involve far reaching changes to business models, professional practices, roles, ethics, products and even challenges to the accepted definitions and understandings of journalism. For Digital Journalism Studies, the field of academic inquiry which explores and examines digital journalism, disruption results in paradigmatic and tectonic shifts in scholarly concerns. It prompts reconsideration of research methods, theoretical analyses and responses (oppositional and consensual) to such changes, which have been described as being akin to 'a moment of mind-blowing uncertainty'.

Routledge's new book series, *Disruptions: Studies in Digital Journalism*, seeks to capture, examine and analyse these moments of exciting and explosive professional and scholarly innovation which characterize developments in the day-to-day practice of journalism in an age of digital media, and which are articulated in the newly emerging academic discipline of Digital Journalism Studies.

Journalism Education for the Digital Age
Promises, Perils, and Possibilities
Brian Creech

Transparency and Journalism
A Critical Appraisal of a Disruptive Norm
Michael Karlsson

Reappraising Local and Community News in the UK
Media, Practice and Policy
David Harte and Rachel Matthews

For more information, please visit: www.routledge.com/Disruptions/book-series/DISRUPTDIGJOUR

Transparency and Journalism
A Critical Appraisal of a Disruptive Norm

Michael Karlsson

 Routledge
Taylor & Francis Group

LONDON AND NEW YORK

First published 2022
by Routledge
2 Park Square, Milton Park, Abingdon, Oxon OX14 4RN

and by Routledge
605 Third Avenue, New York, NY 10158

Routledge is an imprint of the Taylor & Francis Group, an informa business

© 2022 Michael Karlsson

British Library Cataloguing-in-Publication Data
A catalogue record for this book is available from the British Library

Library of Congress Cataloging-in-Publication Data
Names: Karlsson, Michael, 1960- author.
Title: Transparency and journalism : a critical appraisal of a disruptive norm / Michael Karlsson.
Description: London ; New York : Routledge, 2022. |
Series: Disruptions : studies in digital journalism | Includes bibliographical references and index.
Identifiers: LCCN 2021015673 | ISBN 9780367356163 (hardback) | ISBN 9781032101057 (paperback) | ISBN 9780429340642 (ebook)
Subjects: LCSH: Journalistic ethics. | Journalism--Philosophy. | Transparency (Philosophy)
Classification: LCC PN4756 .K34 2022 | DDC 174.907--dc23
LC record available at https://lccn.loc.gov/2021015673

ISBN: 978-0-367-35616-3 (hbk)
ISBN: 978-1-032-10105-7 (pbk)
ISBN: 978-0-429-34064-2 (ebk)

DOI: 10.4324/9780429340642

Typeset in Times New Roman
by Taylor & Francis Books

To my parents Berit and Bo-Gösta

Contents

Tables

Preface and acknowledgements

I have spent almost 20 years, first as a PhD student and later a researcher, trying to understand the transition journalism is going through and the role that transparency has played in it. By the early 2000s transparency was a concept that interested me and transparency's role as a new and tangible norm in journalism formed a significant part of my dissertation that I defended in 2006. Some of those ideas were later translated for an international audience and eventually published in journal articles. When I started out, transparency (and digital journalism as a whole) was an obscure topic in the rather marginalized research field of journalism studies. Twenty years later the academic field of journalism studies has several devoted and highly ranked journals reporting its concerns, and transparency has been adopted by major professional organizations and, more broadly, is seen as a key tool to repair and restore failing trust in democratic institutions.

However, my own initial enthusiasm for what can be accomplished with transparency has been curbed as the empirical evidence has trickled in. This book is very much about highlighting and trying to explain this "transparency gap" between promise and outcome. I understand that there might be some people reading this book who may be surprised by its straightforward tone. This is fine with me, but I want to make it clear that I am primarily picking a fight with myself. More specifically, a fight with my own previous understanding of this topic. Nevertheless, I remain convinced there is a role for transparency in journalism, although it might not be what was originally or currently imagined. I use the opportunity that a book provides to increase knowledge of the area, but also to highlight the complexity of the issue and to suggest that there are no easy or simple fixes. In short, this book is my attempt to summarize, critique, and push the transparency research forward. To get this book started and completed I am indebted to many people that are too numerous to list here. However, there are a few who must be mentioned.

First, I would like to thank Routledge for believing in this project and offering me the opportunity to publish a book on this important topic. Professor Bob Franklin contacted me and encouraged me to write a book proposal about transparency and journalism. I am certain that this book would not have been written without him. I also would like to use this space to thank Bob on behalf of myself and many other colleagues of my generation for his mentorship and guidance for us to find our voice in academia. Being the founding editor of *Journalism Studies, Journalism Practice*, and *Digital Journalism*, as well as a driving force behind the *Future of Journalism* conference, Bob has tutored us in how to write articles, review articles, edit special issues, and so much more.

My good friend and fellow colleague at Karlstad University Professor Henrik Örnebring has read the entire book and generously provided swift, ample, and valuable feedback throughout the process. My conversations with Henrik, easily mistaken for a living encyclopaedia, usually end with me thinking either "I had absolutely no idea about that" or "Of course, why did I not figure that out myself". The book would not have been the same without him. I am also grateful to Dr Susanne Almgren, another colleague at Karlstad University, who commented on the book proposal at one of our internal seminars providing important feedback that strengthened my conviction of the necessity to put the discussion about journalistic transparency in a much wider societal context. Associate Professor Magnus Fredriksson at University of Gothenburg put me on the path to discuss the important difference between freedom of information and disclosure transparency and, subsequently, on how transparency always is and must be strategically managed. This, in turn, impinges on how the intentions of the organization are always an underlying factor when the (sceptic) public evaluate trustworthiness. Finally, I would like to thank Professor Lars Nord at Mid Sweden University and my good friend and fellow colleague at Karlstad University Associate Professor Christer Clerwall for our collaboration on the numerous transparency studies that this book rests on.

1 Transparency and its connection to journalism

Transparency in journalism means being open about how news is made. It also involves inviting citizens to monitor and be a part of that process with the purpose of building and maintaining a strong relationship with them, especially concerning trust. The idea is that if you are more transparent over how journalism is made, then people's misunderstandings, misconceptions, and disbelief in journalism will prove unfounded and sway sceptics towards becoming neutrals or even supporters. If you want the short version of journalism and transparency, well, there you have it. For this to happen, journalism needs to change the way it works in terms of skills, practices, and routines, aligning it with the normative idea of transparency. Should journalism follow suit, then transparency will have disrupted both journalism's normative outlook and the way it works. Transparency, therefore, promises or threatens to change how journalism views itself, its place in the world, and how it creates knowledge about the world. There are already signs that journalism has begun to be disrupted by this norm as transparency even now occupies a central place in journalism practice and journalism studies as a topic worthy of consideration. But it is also a question of how much journalism has changed and whether transparency works as intended.

The rest of this book provides much more detail beyond the brief summary above. The book also complicates, questions, and provides some evidence that there is currently limited support for the view that transparency can fix journalism's broken relationships with the public. Further, it also suggests that algorithmic decision-making, currently on the rise in journalism, makes transparency even more far-fetched. It even proposes the idea that transparency cannot lead to trust since the concepts conflict with each other. But let us not get too far ahead of the story and instead turn our attention to the contemporary mainstream debate on transparency.

DOI: 10.4324/9780429340642-1

The role of transparency in relation to journalism is usually considered an issue of journalistic self-interest, and whether this will make it more accessible and credible to the audience in order to sustain or improve the legitimacy of the journalistic institution, not forgetting support for the business of news. This is the key focus of the debate and hence also this book. But the transparency debate can also be considered from the perspective of viewing journalism as an intermediary between the government and the governed (i.e. the public). Liberal philosophers (see Fenster, 2006, p. 895ff) emphasize publicity as a prerequisite of transparency as a democratic necessity (an argument to be extended in Chapter 2). This publicity can of course be achieved by government itself, but in reality, the public has obtained its information from news media and, increasingly, from non-journalistic arbitrators. Thus, opacity in the intermediary regarding, for instance, where the information comes from can also obscure the public's insight into the government or the government's attempts to explain and justify its decisions (Fenster, 2006). Consequently, there is also the larger issue of democratic accountability at stake in the debate on journalism and transparency in addition to journalism and its legitimacy.

This first chapter provides background and context concerning how transparency made its way into journalism practice and studies and the purpose it is supposed to serve. It returns to some of the accounts offered by journalists and scholars in the early 2000s that focused on the declining trust in, and consumption of, journalism. There were many advocates from both the academy (including the proponent of this book[1]) and the journalism industry touting transparency as a remedy for the decline (Lasorsa, 2012; Phillips, 2012), not least because the ideal of transparency fitted neatly with the affordances of burgeoning digital media (e.g. unlimited space, hyperlinks, interactivity) (Karlsson, 2011). This chapter develops by revisiting some of the key claims that also set up the path for much of the research to follow, thus explaining why much contemporary research has ended up where it is. The subsequent section argues that there is only a weak theoretical and empirical foundation that transparency will serve the purpose that protagonists suggest, prompting the need to look beyond the journalistic field and explore the roots of transparency and its proposed function in those fields. A broader review of transparency in other fields is presented in Chapter 2. This chapter's third section offers a perspective on understanding how transparency is enacted in journalistic practice, describing different ways in which journalists can be transparent and what they do when they are conducting journalism transparently. The final section opens with a brief overview of theoretical perspectives – institutional theory and Goffman's theory of social interaction – that inform the book. The final section also offers a summary of the structure of the book and a short note on each of the six chapters.

Transparency: Essence, purpose, and how it made its way into journalism

If there is a single word that previous research has used to explain transparency it would be "openness" (Heim & Craft, 2020; Karlsson, 2010; Plaisance, 2007; Vos & Craft, 2017). Openness here refers to generally opening up the black box (Singer, 2005) that used to be the news industry generally and the newsroom specifically. According to a range of researchers, journalism has been sealed off to the outside, including the public it is supposed to serve and be accountable to – a black box fortress going by the name "newsroom", from which news appears to spontaneously emerge at regular intervals (Deuze, 2003; Gillmor, 2004; Karlsson, 2011; Singer, 2005). According to Singer's observation (2005, p. 179), the news media are among the opaquest industries and news people have not been particularly keen to "let the public in on how the sausage is made". Had the posture been given a sausage-appropriate slogan it might have been "Eat it or beat it". And beat it the public gradually did, although it remains to be seen whether this is due to the lack of exhaustive sausage-making knowledge or something else. It is my hope that this book helps inform that debate.

The decline in the relationship between journalism and the public is visible in at least three different areas: first, the diminishing news consumption affecting revenue and advertising rates (Kurpius et al., 2010; Pickard & Williams, 2014; Thurman & Myllylahti, 2009); second, the reality that trust and credibility ratings are going down among the (American) public, affecting not only news consumption but also the legitimacy of journalism as a social institution (Brenan, 2019; Pew Research Center, 2013; Newman et al., 2019); and third, the fact that the objectivity norm, a mainstay in high-modern journalism for decades, is being questioned by insiders (Vos & Craft, 2017) as a viable long-term norm and needs to be replaced or supplemented by a better option (cue transparency).

As the relationship deteriorates further, the need for solutions only becomes more urgent.

Transparency can, at least partially, be a response to these developments and its main purpose is to rehabilitate journalism's declining relationship, especially in the US, with the public – a response that has been brandished by academics, debaters, and journalists alike. From relative obscurity, transparency was picked up by journalists, debaters, and scholars in the early 2000s. In the first edition of their milestone book *The Elements of Journalism*, Kovach and Rosenstiel (2001, p. 78) proposed that journalists should "[be as] transparent as possible about [their] methods and motives". By the time the second edition of the book was out (Kovach & Rosenstiel, 2007), they had noted that transparency had been given even more prominence in the field and this was reflected in their extended treatment of the topic as well. In 2004, J.D. Lasica suggested in the *Online Journalism Review* that the transparency found in blogs helped to explain the fact that they were perceived as more credible than news media, and that mainstream journalists might benefit from learning from their "cutting-edge cousins" (Lasica, 2004).

In the summer of 2004, 24 media executives, journalists, and consultants gathered at the Eighth Annual Aspen Institute Conference on Journalism and Society "to examine the policies and practices that enable ethical entanglements to occur and to explore strategies by which news organizations can strengthen the public's confidence in the integrity of their journalism" (Ziomek, 2005, p. v). Charles Firestone, the executive director of the Aspen Institute Communications and Society Program, challenged the participants with the question "With the changes in communications technology, can you afford not to be transparent?" (Ziomek, 2005, p. vi). The participants at the conferences responded unanimously that transparency is key for the industry, practitioners, and the public to come together and rebuild trust in the media. The counselling to the journalistic field boiled down to: "Good journalism should be as transparent as practical" (Ziomek, 2005, p. vi).

For Plaisance (2007, p. 193), transparency could also be used as a tool for credibility in interactions with the public: "For journalists confronted by an often hostile public, transparency is more than academic; it is an essential element of credibility". David Weinberger suggested in 2009 that transparency was the new objectivity because "...we want, need, can have and expect transparency. Transparency – the embedded ability to see through the published draft – often gives us more reason to believe a report than the claim of objectivity did" (Weinberger, 2009). Although there is no lack of conviction in the argument, it is peculiarly vague who the "we" are.

But there have also been sceptical and critical voices regarding what transparency can bring to journalism. Allen (2008) feared that it can be used to dodge criticism and defend the institution rather than to change it. In 2006, Rachel Smolkin had already expressed her scepticism by comparing journalists' commitment to transparency with the belief that healing crystals can solve all problems (Smolkin, 2006). In an almost identical remark in 2013, media ethicist Stephen Ward criticized the optimism over transparency that accredited it with magical powers to restore democracy (Ward, 2013). Instead, Ward put out a warning that transparency is insufficient to ensure ethical conduct and might lead to excessive caution among management. Despite these objections and, as we shall see later in Chapter 3, there being little to show in terms of substantial effects, transparency has gradually been incorporated by the news media, the journalistic profession, and academia alike.

By the mid-2010s, transparency had been institutionalized in the sense that it had become officially embraced as a way of doing journalism properly. Thus, it took roughly a decade between the point in time when the term first began to appear in serious discussion and when it had become amalgamated by journalism. Perhaps the most significant sign of transparency's grip is its inclusion as an acknowledged professional norm (Heim & Craft, 2020; Vos & Craft, 2017). The US Society of Professional Journalists (SPJ) added transparency to their Code of Ethics in the latest revision (in 2014). More specifically, a whole section, "Be accountable and transparent", is devoted to it and here it is explained that "[e]thical journalism means taking responsibility for one's work and explaining one's decisions to the public" (Society of Professional Journalists, n.d.). The Radio Television Digital News Association (RTDNA) revised their code of ethics in 2015 to incorporate transparency (Heim & Craft, 2020). They expounded the role of transparency as: "provid[ing] the public with the means to assess credibility and to determine who deserves trust". Elaborating how journalists should work with transparency, they portend that "[e]ffectively explaining editorial decisions and processes does not mean making excuses. Transparency requires reflection, reconsideration and honest openness to the possibility that an action, however well intended, was wrong" (The Radio Television Digital News Association, n.d.).

Journalists' organizations revising their codes of ethics is not the only sign of transparency's spread. The 200-plus-page report *Crisis in Democracy: Renewing Trust in America* from the Knight Commission on Trust, Media and Democracy advocates that journalists "practice radical transparency" as the number one recommendation to restore trust in journalism (The Aspen Institute, 2019, p. 7). In the edited volume *The New Ethics of Journalism: Principles for the 21st Century* (2014), editors Kelly McBride and Tom Rosenstiel gather prominent researchers, journalists, and debaters to consider and update journalistic ethics. Through the stewardship of The Poynter Institute they seek to distil the core principles of journalism into a book for contemporary journalism. One new key ethical principle is transparency "…because it is so essential a part of how modern journalism attains credibility" (McBride & Rosenstiel, 2014, p. 2). A third of the book is dedicated to transparency and "learning the transparency habit" (McBride & Rosenstiel, 2014, p. 89). Here they detail experiences from the journalistic field that transparency is a way to open up journalism to the audience so that this will improve journalists' standings as "...there was a clear sense that if we [i.e. journalists, authors' remark] tell the audience how and why we do things, they won't assign spurious motives to our actions". McBride and Rosenstiel also suggest that they underestimated what information would be interesting to the audience and that their efforts at transparency were hampered by capacity rather than by demand. In other words, to summarize the overarching argument, there is a requirement for transparency by the audience, and if journalists find the time and learn how to be transparent, they will be rewarded by trust. Therefore, transparency is an ethical habit well worth pursuing, and should it be achieved, rewards will be aplenty for everyone.

The fragile theoretical and empirical foundation of transparency in journalism

Despite the extensive institutional embrace of transparency as *the* norm that will guide journalism in the future and make it more trustworthy and relevant to the public, there is in fact both little empirical support that increased transparency produces the desired effects and a weak theoretical foundation for the concept itself in journalism studies.[2] Journalism practitioners and scholars are not making a great effort to move outside their field and connect to the transparency debates that have been going on in other areas of the humanities and social sciences. Transparency and its role as a remedy for decreasing trust in news media is an appealing and neat idea. However, its introduction into journalism studies and practice did not come from a solid theoretical and empirical foundation but largely from journalism and industry insiders who were looking for a way to change or tweak journalism to save it. This perspective has so far dominated the debate. While this is a perfectly legitimate approach to journalism and transparency, it is *a* research approach but not necessarily the most appropriate one. Quite a lot of the early debate and research provided anecdotal evidence of its success, celebrating editorial policies that embraced the norm, lamenting editorial policies that did not, and repeating the underlying assumptions articulated within the field. Critical perspectives were rare, the actual transparency performance was largely unmeasured, and input from the public was missing. To be somewhat callous, an overall impression of the discussion on transparency so far, and especially in the earlier years, is that transparency was invented by journalism and is a success story waiting to happen if just done right.

Yet journalism at the turn of the millennium was neither the first time nor place to consider the role of transparency in communication, as it has roots in political theory. In journalism studies the reasoning behind, and expectations regarding, what role transparency may serve have primarily been philosophically anchored (if at all) in Kantian ethics (Plaisance, 2007). Plaisance's (2007, p. 188) proposed definition of transparent behaviour is a "conduct that presumes an openness in communication and serves a reasonable expectation of forthright exchange when parties have a legitimate stake in the possible outcomes or effects of the communicative act". Furthermore, Plaisance (2007, p. 187) points to the relationship between rational and autonomous actors implying that both must have an opportunity to act on their own: "Transparent interaction is what allows us as rational, autonomous beings to assess each other's behavior". In short, transparent journalism should rest on the notion that concerned parties have a stake in the outcome of the communication and that the communication itself should be easy to understand, open, honest, and reciprocal. When communication has these qualities, both the public and journalists[3] can make rational decisions on their own as to whether it meets agreed standards. This line of thinking is clearly discernible in the above quotes from the SPJ, RTDNA, and other actors. We will return to philosophical and political theories on what transparency is and what purpose it has, and its connection to liberal democratic theory, in Chapter 2.

Transparency as ritual in journalistic practice

If transparency is openness, it remains necessary to elucidate what constitutes openness and in what ways journalism can be open. Transparency in the abstract needs to be translated into daily journalistic work, to be ritualized and normalized (Karlsson, 2010; Tuchman, 1972). A journalism that is transparent will entail a need not only for different norms and ideals but also for altering other types of journalistic skills and practices guided by said norms and ideals. Otherwise, it would not be a linkage between lofty institution-wide ideals and localized everyday journalism (Mellado, 2015). If skills and practices do not change, not much will happen, either with the journalistic output or with the relationship with the public. Furthermore, it if is supposed to make any difference to the audience, transparent journalism must be perceptibly distinctive from non-transparent journalism. In other words, for journalism to be transparent it must appropriate succinct ways of conducting journalism "transparently", that is, "rituals that can be used in everyday journalistic work and be communicated to, understood and accepted as journalistic routines by the audience and peers" (Karlsson, 2010, p. 536). In performing these rituals in public, journalists illustrate, justify, and perpetuate the legitimate ways of doing journalism, assuming that the public and other constituents accept these.

If transparency is not translated into performable rituals that are acceptable to the public, it would be impossible to decide whether a piece of journalism was transparent or not and whether this had any implications for perceived credibility from the perspective of the public. In short, a transparent journalism is conducted differently to a non-transparent journalism. Or, posed as a question, what should journalists do differently to be transparent? Elsewhere (Karlsson, 2010, 2020) I have proposed that there are at least three theoretically and empirically distinct forms of transparency: *disclosure* and *participatory transparency*, and later *ambient transparency*.

Disclosure transparency (Karlsson, 2010, p. 537) comprises forms of openness where news producers "explain and [are] open about the way news is selected and produced", and thus make journalistic routines discernible. This can encompass explaining the gathering, selection, and processing of news. This form of transparency presupposes common faith and shared values regarding what constitutes "good journalism" between journalists and the public (as suggested by Plaisance's definition above): for instance, that accuracy is an important trait of journalism, that errors should be avoided but honest mistakes can happen, and that corrections are an appropriate way to address the misstep. Although the public are an important part of disclosure transparency, they are not required to play an active role, but can serve as a distant and silent reminder that journalism needs to perform well according to agreed-upon standards.

Participatory transparency (Karlsson, 2010, p. 538) comprises forms of openness where the users are "…being invited to participate in different stages in the news production process". This dimension of transparency is tied to the *forthright exchange* emphasized by Plaisance, where the common platform is extended beyond faith and values to include frequent and easily accomplished exchange between journalists and the public. This can be materialized in the form of direct contributions to the news stories in, for example, the form of eyewitness reports, embedded tweets or You-Tube videos, and photos sent to the newsroom. It can also be monitoring, commenting on, and criticizing news reports in commentary fields or on social media. All forms of feedback that individually or collectively impinge on the journalistic work and how the news story in question – or future news stories – appears are forms of participatory transparency.

Finally, there is, what I have tentatively labelled, *ambient transparency*. Ambient transparency (Karlsson, 2020, p. 1808) comprises techniques or tools that news producers add "in the vicinity of (news) content making it possible for news consumers to evaluate and form new meanings of news stories, through the association of content with the provided context". These tools can be hyperlinks, various graphical markers indicating what section or genre the news story is published in, or whether it is a news story, a regular ad or native advertising, or the personal opinions of journalists. In short, "[a]mbient transparency techniques add information around the edges of news stories but disregard the public inside the frame of the news stories, and do not explain the content per se, unlike participatory and disclosure transparency" (Karlsson, 2020, p. 1808f). This form of transparency is not explicitly covered in Plaisance's definition. However, as a suggestion, it can be seen as a form of "openness in communication" as it puts a specific piece of information (e.g. a news story) into a wider context that improves the public's chances of assessing the behaviour and drawing rational conclusions about both the news story and the journalism providing it.

In the literature, disclosure forms of transparency are the ones most frequently and openly mentioned when "transparency" is brought up. Nevertheless, the theoretical definitions (see above and in Chapter 2) typically involve a reciprocal relation between an organization and its public. Furthermore, a factor analysis in the above-mentioned survey study from Sweden (Karlsson, 2020) found that the public also view transparency as the three aforementioned distinct yet linked dimensions. Whether this is applicable beyond the Swedish context remains to be discovered in future research.

Theoretical points of departure influencing the book

While this book focuses on the role of transparency in journalism and will not discuss at great length various grand social theories and their applicability to journalism, I think it is important to say something about the theoretical backdrop that informs this book. In particular, there are two theoretical approaches that have served as an inspiration, points of reference and analytical tools, namely institutional theory and Goffman's theory of social interaction (Goffman, 2004).

Institutional theory is a fruitful approach to understanding the interaction between factors at the macro and micro level of journalism where the former shapes the latter (see Carlson, 2017; DiMaggio & Powell, 1983; Lowrey, 2011; Meyer & Rowan, 1977; Örnebring & Karlsson, forthcoming; Thornton & Ocasio, 2008; Vos, 2020 for a more extensive and detailed account on institutional theory and journalism). For the purposes of this book, institutional theory is pertinent for a few reasons.

First, it identifies a social institution (e.g. journalism, education, healthcare, law enforcement, etc.) as an actor that has legitimate authority over a particular domain. In journalism's case, this is, in short, the role of an independent intermediary that helps citizens to understand the governing of society by informing them enough to enable them to make autonomous choices in elections and hold people in power accountable. This is the current self-articulated social mission of journalism and it is important to understand what any discussion of norms, practices, and skills in general, and transparency in particular, has to relate to. But the social mission must be manifest somehow.

Thus, second, for any social institution there are certain homogeneous beliefs, norms, practices, ideals, and rules on how to do and, equally importantly, not to do things. Meyer and Rowan (1977, p. 341) explain the path towards institutionalization as involving "...the processes by which social processes, obligations, or actualities come to take on a rule-like status in social thought and action". These rules are recognized both within and outside (by various constituents, most crucially the public) the boundaries of the institution and guide expectations on how both organizations and individual members within the institution must or should behave. With regard to journalism, this could, for instance, be the extensive use of several sources to inform the news, while simultaneously making sure that the sources do not have too much influence over how the news is framed. It can be adhering to the codes of ethics, or the materiality of the printing press as a strong metaphor for journalism as a whole, or the press conference as a place where important things are uttered to a select gathering of worthy professionals, etc. The key point is that the institution *is* these expressions as "[a]n institution is constituted by routinized practices, implicit and explicit rules, and explicit norms" (Vos, 2020, p. 736; see also Thornton & Ocasio, 2008).

Third, these ways of doing things properly are to a large extent taken for granted, in that they do not need to be explained or justified on a regular basis. Instead, there is consensus on "how things get done around here", a ceremonial conformity (Christensen & Cornelissen, 2015; Meyer & Rowan, 1977). The term "ceremonial conformity" is quite genius since it at the same time points to the need for conformism across the institution, and the fact that the conformism is manifested in quite unreflective practice. Not knowing the naturalized state of things by asking, for instance, why sources are needed in journalism would only expose how much of an outsider one would be, or, in the case of transparency, to advocate it 30 years ago, question its use today, or having an as yet unknown position in 10 or 20 years' time.

Fourth, since the key norms, routines, and practices must be shared and enacted throughout the institution for the institution to manifest and reproduce itself, they can be studied empirically. Such studies could then indicate the extent to which an old norm, objectivity, is on its way out and whether a new norm, transparency, is on the rise (see Vos, 2020 and Vos & Craft, 2017 for a more detailed argument).

Fifth, the authority and legitimacy that derives from the recognized and taken-for-granted ways of conducting journalism both enable and constrain the behaviour of individual journalists. The rank-and-file journalists cannot conduct journalism in too much of a non-institutional way without being reprimanded or even being declared a pariah and expelled from the community. Should an individual member of the institution wander off too much, the leading members of the social institution will go to great pains to explain how this is an atypical behaviour in their attempts to defend and repair the legitimacy of the institution as a whole (i.e. paradigm repair as discussed by, amongst others, Bennett et al., 1985 and Hindman, 2005).

Sixth, and finally, although there is a strong inclination toward path dependency and doing things in the old ways, the institution can be challenged and changed. If the challenge is successful, there will be new ways of making journalism proper and, eventually, the new ways of doing things will be codified into a code of ethics and become acclimatized as transparency arguably was in the period 2014–2015. One way of explaining changes in institutions is that, in their efforts to uphold or boost their own legitimacy, they "borrow elements from institutions that already enjoy social legitimacy" (Vos, 2020, p. 741). Especially in times of uncertainty, organizations might employ mimetic isomorphism and model themselves on other seemingly successful organizations (DiMaggio & Powell, 1983). Hence, to understand the place of transparency in journalism we may be well-served by investigating the transparency discourse in adjacent social institutions (more on this in Chapter 2).

Taken together, from an institutional theory perspective, the claim that transparency is a key ethical dimension of contemporary journalism is testament to a remarkable institutional change in journalism. It can therefore be argued that transparency is a key component in journalism's attempt to "creat[e] new practices, norms, structures, and relationships [itself]" (Picard, 2014, p. 279) and thus reinstitutionalize itself with new rules in the face of the unprecedented disruption that has marked the industry in the last 20 or so years. This argument is illustrated by previous quotes from industry leaders, professional organizations and distinguished members of the field who pay homage to the centrality of transparency in building authority and legitimacy (e.g. as a tool to get the public to trust journalism more). From this explicit commitment to transparency, it follows that it is also something that journalists across the field can do, should do, must do, or at least have a very good explanation for why they are not doing it. Transparency has become a point of reference, a centre of gravity for any debate about journalism. Thus, when the journalistic institution at large has committed to the transparency norm through codes of ethics and public pledges by industry leaders, it will come with a psychological and social cost for individual journalists to question and deviate from it *regardless* of how effective it is in practice – a discussion that we will return to in Chapter 5.

In the literature this commitment to transparency is visible in terms such as "the transparency habit" (McBride & Rosenstiel, 2014), "the spirit of transparency" (Kovach & Rosenstiel, 2007) or the call for journalists to "practice radical transparency" by the Knight Commission on Trust, Media and Democracy (The Aspen Institute, 2019). These pledges to adopt transparency by influential actors within the field are powerful and convincing while at the same time lacking precision and systematic empirical support. It is, on the one hand, difficult to understand what, for instance, a radical transparency is and what effects it will have compared to a mere mainstream transparency, laconic transparency, or other forms of transparency. On the other hand, the elevated and celebrated position of an abstruse concept makes it difficult to criticize or scrutinize (Christensen & Cornelissen, 2015). The key observation to bring with us in the rest of the book is that transparency is one of the – if not *the* – "natural" points of departure in the normative debate on contemporary and future journalism and that leading members of the institution itself embrace it.

Institutional theory is valuable in pointing out that there needs to be some internal consistency in journalism with regard to beliefs, routines, and practices, and that it is possible and necessary to study this empirically. However, it is not as useful in explaining or studying *how* these beliefs, routines, and practices are enacted. Luckily, Goffman's dramaturgical approach is suitable for understanding and analysing how transparency is enacted in practice at the micro level. Expressed simply, in one way or another, journalists are on a stage where they have to perform transparency to the public, who can either be indifferent to it, challenge it or accept it (Craft et al., 2016; Karlsson, 2011; Karlsson & Clerwall, 2019). The more previously hidden parts of news production are moved to the stage, or new aspects are introduced (e.g. user participation), the more open, and hence transparent, the performance becomes (see also Karlsson, 2011).

As stated above, without the acknowledgement and acceptance from the public that a performance is transparent, and that this performance is better (whatever that is taken to mean) than a non-transparent performance, there cannot be any effect on public trust in journalism. To be able to investigate whether this is happening, it is necessary to identify some key components in the performance. They are, arguably, the stage, the actors (performers and audience), the script (or play), the aesthetics and delivery of the play and, finally, the effect. These components will be developed in a dedicated section in Chapter 2 detailing the building blocks of a proposed model, tentatively labelled "the performative transparency communication model" (drawing quite heavily on Goffman).

The imagined audience, structure, and content of the book

In writing this book I imagined four main audiences: fellow researchers, students, media practitioners, and the interested public. I hope they will find something of interest, something to agree with, and something to disagree with. My ambition has been to write an informed yet critical account of a research area that I have been following and contributing to for nearly two decades. I deliberately, as the subtitle of the book suggests, set out to present a critical appraisal of the topic since it has many supporters but very few critics. An issue that is so tantalizing and has so much promise to affect so much must be met with critical scrutiny and questions about its limitations and flaws, otherwise it will not be possible to see what it can and cannot accomplish. Furthermore, it may stand in the way of other, yet-to-be-discovered measures that better address the issues that transparency is predicted to fix. The book is structured as follows.

Chapter 1 has aimed to provide a short introduction to what transparency in journalism is essentially about as well as a brief review of the recent history of transparency, summarizing the contemporary mainstream transparency debate and providing definitions of different kinds of transparency. The chapter also intends to inform the reader about theoretical perspectives supporting the outlook in this book.

Chapter 2 places journalistic transparency into a wider context by bringing in perspectives from primarily political theory, but also economy, healthcare, international relations, and organizational studies. This chapter argues, first, that transparency in journalism is in some critical ways fundamentally different from other fields, especially with regard to some structural features (e.g. they do not serve the same purpose or have similar preconditions). But the chapter also argues that there are substantial overlaps with other fields, not least at the operational level where transparency is supposed to happen. Regardless of what field transparency takes place in, there is a common idea of how it will work – an implicit theory of transparency. In this chapter, I put forward building blocks that together crudely constitute what I tentatively call "the performative transparency model of communication".

In Chapter 1 I have detailed the hopes that are tied to transparency – that it provides a path for journalism to find a new way to earn trust from citizens and through that maintain social authority and legitimacy. Chapter 3 takes stock of that prediction and offers a review of much of the research that has been done so far in journalism studies. The focus is on empirical studies and the chapter is organized into three sections – the production, content, and reception of transparency. There are a couple of takeaways from this chapter. First, despite the relative importance that has been given to transparency and the expectations tied to it, there is surprisingly little empirical research, especially when it comes to analysis of how transparency is expressed in day-to-day journalism. Second, the research that has been done so far shows there is little interest from either journalists or the public.

Chapter 4 takes a closer look at the transparency issues that arise when software and algorithms occupy an ever-increasing space in journalism. In addition to algorithms occupying a larger space in journalism, their introduction leads to journalism being less an issue for journalists and more of an issue for algorithms themselves, as well as programmers, designers and others who create, maintain, and oversee algorithms. This chapter illustrates how algorithms provide new opportunities for transparency, as well as challenges, and another set of black boxes inside the journalistic black box as well as inside non-journalistic black boxes.

Chapter 5 entertains the idea that the underlying assumptions and points of departure in the debate about transparency in journalism are off the mark, and poses the soul-searching question: Is this about sausage dockets and sausage-making-knowledge in the first place? Or framed a tad more seriously: Is transparency the answer to journalism's trust troubles? In this chapter I return to the theoretical discussion introduced in Chapters 1 and 2 concerning what transparency really is and what it can help accomplish. Amongst other things, there will be a focus on the cost/benefit problem, which is rarely discussed. The necessity of professional discretion in decision-making is contrasted with the openness of transparency. Related to this, regardless of how much of journalism is made open, there is still something that is concealed, and the public is almost always at a disadvantage in accessing information beyond what is provided by journalists or other intermediaries. Thus, the openness offered is yet more second-hand information with associated issues of concealment. Furthermore, a fundamental conflict between transparency and trust is highlighted. I also make the proposition that associating transparency with openness is misguided and it would be more accurate to view transparency as strategically managed visibility. Lastly, the disjointedness between transparency in theory and transparency in practice is discussed through the lens of institutional theory.

Closing the book, Chapter 6 departs from the assumption that transparency can still serve a function for journalism despite the discouraging results reported in Chapter 3 and the theoretical interventions in Chapter 5. It proposes some scenarios where transparency can serve a bigger role than current research has uncovered. In line with this, several strands are presented where future research is needed.

Notes

1 My thinking on the issue has evolved because of the empirical studies that I and colleagues have conducted as well as reading up on other fields. I still think there is a role for transparency to play but it is smaller than currently understood. I also think that transparency is a poor remedy for the key problem it is supposed to solve – converting people that mistrust journalism. Hopefully, this book can provide an explanation as to why this move is logical.
2 To the best of my knowledge, the first empirical study actually measuring the effect transparency has on credibility was published in 2014 and gave little reason to cheer (more on this in Chapter 3). This is the very same year that the SPJ changed their ethical guidelines to include transparency. The (lack of) theoretical connection between transparency and trust is extensively discussed in Chapter 5.
3 And other actors too, but they are not at the centre of this discussion as transparency is primarily framed as a tool for the journalism–public relationship.

References

Allen, D. S. (2008). The trouble with transparency. *Journalism Studies*, 9(3), 323–340. https://doi.org/10.1080/14616700801997224.
Bennett, L., Gresset, L., & Haltom, W. (1985). Repairing the news: A case study of the news paradigm. *Journal of Communication*, 35(2), 50–68.

Brenan, M. (2019). *Americans' Trust in Mass Media Edges Down to 41%*. https://news.gallup.com/poll/267047/americans-trust-mass-media-edges-down.aspx.

Carlson, M. (2017). *Journalistic Authority Legitimizing News in the Digital Era*. Columbia University Press.

Christensen, L. T., & Cornelissen, J. (2015). Organizational transparency as myth and metaphor. *European Journal of Social Theory*, 18(2), 132–149. https://doi.org/10.1177/1368431014555256.

Craft, S., Vos, T. P., & David Wolfgang, J. (2016). Reader comments as press criticism: Implications for the journalistic field. *Journalism*, 17(6), 677–693. https://doi.org/10.1177/1464884915579332.

Deuze, M. (2003). The web and its journalisms: Considering the consequences of different types of news media online. *New Media & Society*, 5(2), 203–230. https://doi.org/10.1177/1461444803005002004.

DiMaggio, P. J., & Powell, W. W. (1983). The iron cage revisited: Institutional isomorphism and collective rationality in organizational fields. *American Sociological Review*, 48(2), 147–160.

Fenster, M. (2006). The opacity of transparency. *Iowa Law Review*, 91(3), 885–949.

Gillmor, D. (2004). *We the Media: Grassroots Journalism By the People, For the People*. O'Reilly Media.

Goffman, E. (2004). *Jaget och maskerna: En studie i vardagslivets dramatik*. Norstedts.

Heim, K., & Craft, S. (2020). Transparency in journalism: Meanings, merits, and risks. In L. Wilkins & C. Christians (Eds.), *The Routledge Handbook of Mass Media Ethics* (pp. 308–320). Routledge.

Hindman, E. (2005). Jayson Blair, *The New York Times*, and paradigm repair. *Journal of Communication*, 55(2), 225–241. http://onlinelibrary.wiley.com/doi/10.1111/j.1460-2466.2005.tb02669.x/abstract.

Karlsson, M. (2010). Rituals of transparency: Evaluating online news outlets' uses of transparency rituals in the United States, United Kingdom and Sweden. *Journalism Studies*, 11(4), 535–545. www.informaworld.com/smpp/content~db=all~content=a924114735.

Karlsson, M. (2011). The immediacy of online news, the visibility of journalistic processes and a restructuring of journalistic authority. *Journalism*, 12(3), 279–295. https://doi.org/10.1177/1464884910388223.

Karlsson, M. (2020). Dispersing the opacity of transparency in journalism on the appeal of different forms of transparency to the general public. *Journalism Studies*, 21(3), 1795–1814. https://doi.org/10.1080/1461670X.2020.1790028.

Karlsson, M., & Clerwall, C. (2019). Cornerstones in journalism: According to citizens. *Journalism Studies*, 20(8), 1184–1199. https://doi.org/10.1080/1461670X.2018.1499436.

Kovach, B., & Rosenstiel, T. (2001). *The Elements of Journalism: What News-people Should Know and the Public Should Expect* (1st edn). Crown Publishers.

Kovach, B., & Rosenstiel, T. (2007). *The Elements of Journalism: What News-people Should Know and the Public Should Expect* (2nd edn). Three Rivers Press.

Kurpius, D. D., Metzgar, E. T., & Rowley, K. M. (2010). Sustaining hyperlocal media. *Journalism Studies*, 11(3), 359–376. https://doi.org/10.1080/14616700 903429787.

Lasica, J. D. (2004). *Transparency Begets Trust in the Ever-Expanding Blogosphere.* www.ojr.org/ojr/technology/1092267863.php?_cf_chl_captcha_tk__=b83edf3a 84a74488828a7d8c2743d84d01b86df8-1615194466-0-Aayj8VnPgYH5aDPemL TTSJdzShfrcQ3ItNtfjjB6BJQ1Bqzv46bKTxLUZyjZgrXP_23_1r_1toZNYdj5f Wb64TsXnSb6ndiK_mnLWlkLJ4EKV0y1wbR5_lzUr_H2IVChEw.

Lasorsa, D. (2012). Transparency and other journalistic norms on twitter. *Journalism Studies*, 13(2), 402–417. https://doi.org/10.1080/1461670X.2012.657909.

Lowrey, W. (2011). Institutionalism, news organizations and innovation. *Journalism Studies*, 12(1), 64–79. https://doi.org/10.1080/1461670X.2010.511954.

McBride, K., & Rosenstiel, T. (2014). *The New Ethics of Journalism: Principles for the 21st Century.* Sage.

Mellado, C. (2015). Professional roles in news content: Six dimensions of journalistic role performance. *Journalism Studies*, 16(4), 596–614. https://doi. org/10.1080/1461670X.2014.922276.

Meyer, J. W., & Rowan, B. (1977). Institutionalized organizations: Formal structure as myth and ceremony. *American Journal of Sociology*, 83(2), 340–363.

Newman, N., Fletcher, R., Kalogeropoulos, A., & Nielsen, R. K. (2019). *Reuters Institute Digital News Report 2019.* https://reutersinstitute.politics. ox.ac.uk/sites/default/files/2019-06/DNR_2019_FINAL_0.pdf.

Örnebring, H., & Karlsson, M. (forthcoming). *Journalistic Autonomy: A Genealogy of a Concept.*

Pew Research Center. (2013). *Amid Criticism, Support for Media's "Watchdog" Role Stands Out.* www.pewresearch.org/politics/2013/08/08/amid-criticism -support-for-medias-watchdog-role-stands-out/.

Phillips, A. (2012). Transparency and the ethics of new journalism. In P. Lee-Wright, A. Phillips, & T. Witschge (Eds.), *Changing Journalism* (pp. 135–148). Routledge.

Picard, R. G. (2014). Twilight or new dawn of journalism? *Digital Journalism*, 2(3), 273–283. https://doi.org/10.1080/1461670X.2014.895530.

Pickard, V., & Williams, A. T. (2014). Salvation or folly? The promises and perils of digital paywalls. *Digital Journalism*, 2(2), 195–213. https://doi.org/ 10.1080/21670811.2013.865967.

Plaisance, P. L. (2007). Transparency: An assessment of the Kantian roots of a key element in media ethics practice. *Journal of Mass Media Ethics*, 22(2–3), 187–207. https://doi.org/10.1080/08900520701315855.

Singer, J. (2005). The political j-blogger: "Normalizing" a new media form to fit old norms and practices. *Journalism*, 6(2), 173–198. https://doi.org/10. 1177/1464884905051009.

Smolkin, R. (2006). *Too Transparent?* https://ajrarchive.org/article.asp?id= 4073&id=4073.

Society of Professional Journalists. (n.d.). *SPJ Code of Ethics.* https://doi.org/ 10.1017/cbo9780511811975.016.

The Aspen Institute. (2019). *The Report of the Knight Commission on Trust, Media and Democracy: Crisis in Democracy: Renewing Trust in America.* http://as.pn/trust.

The Radio Television Digital News Association. (n.d.). *RTDNA Code of Ethics.* www.rtdna.org/content/rtdna_code_of_ethics.

Thornton, P. H., & Ocasio, W. (2008). Institutional logics. In R. Greenwood, C. Oliver, R. Suddaby & K. Sahlin (Eds.), *The SAGE Handbook of Organizational Institutionalism* (pp. 99–128). Sage. https://doi.org/10.4135/9781849200387.n4.

Thurman, N., & Myllylahti, M. (2009). Taking the paper out of news. *Journalism Studies*, 10(5), 691–708. https://doi.org/10.1080/14616700902812959.

Tuchman, G. (1972). Objectivity as a strategic ritual. *The American Journal of Sociology*, 77(4), 660–679.

Vos, T. (2020). Journalism as institution. In H. Örnebring (Ed.), *The Oxford Encyclopedia of Journalism Studies* (pp. 736–750). Oxford University Press.

Vos, T. P., & Craft, S. (2017). The discursive construction of journalistic transparency. *Journalism Studies*, 18(12), 1505–1522. https://doi.org/10.1080/1461670X.2015.1135754.

Ward, S. (2013). *Why Hyping Transparency Distorts Journalism Ethics.* http://mediashift.org/2013/11/why-hyping-transparency-distorts-journalism-ethics/.

Weinberger, D. (2009). Transparency: The new objectivity. *KM World*, 18. www.kmworld.com/Articles/Column/David-Weinberger/Transparency-the-new-objectivity-55785.aspx.

Ziomek, J. (2005). *Journalism, Transparency and the Public Trust: A Report of the Eighth Annual Aspen Institute Conference on Journalism and Society.* www.aspeninstitute.org/wp-content/uploads/files/content/docs/cands/JOURTRANSPTEXT.PDF.

2 Journalistic transparency in history and context

This chapter places journalistic transparency in a wider societal and theoretical context. There are two reasons for this: first, journalism studies tend to focus on subjects that journalism practice considers a current problem/solution; second, most of the solutions/problems seem to be aimed at "doing something" with journalism, whether it includes participation, algorithms, or, as in this case, translating transparency into journalistic norms and practices. This means that both scholars and practitioners turn to journalism, to paraphrase Örnebring (2019), to solve journalism's problems instead of looking more broadly in both time and space. There might be lessons to learn about both the benefits and drawbacks of transparency from other fields that journalism studies and practice have yet to discover.

To address this shortfall, this chapter considers discussions and debates around transparency beyond contemporary journalism. It does so in two ways: first, it gauges the historical and philosophical roots of transparency in liberal political theory; second, it reviews how transparency is viewed and used by social institutions other than journalism (primarily politics but also with examples from economy, international relations, healthcare, and organizational studies). The reason for this comparison is the likelihood that the journalistic institution mimics transparency from other social institutions of high public standing since, as pointed out in Chapter 1, institutions "borrow elements from institutions that already enjoy social legitimacy" (Vos, 2020, p. 741; see also DiMaggio & Powell, 1983). Transparency, as we shall see, appeared in other institutions long before it was an issue in journalism. Since transparency was neither invented in journalism nor was it among the first social institutions to adopt it, we need to look to these other fields to see what benefits journalism seeks to reap. We also need to compare differences and similarities between those institutions and journalism.

DOI: 10.4324/9780429340642-2

Consequently this chapter offers a comparison of some fundamental differences and similarities between these other social institutions and journalism to see the extent to which those prerequisites and expressions of transparency are transferable to journalism, and how this impacts on the role transparency can play in journalism. One finding is that regardless of the social institution in question, there is a similar notion of how transparency is supposed to work. I call this "the implicit theory of transparency", and it aligns with a linear and purified (Christensen & Cheney, 2015; Etzioni, 2010; Fenster, 2006) view of communication and its effects.

The final section of the chapter provides a detailed account of, and argument about, what constitutes the building blocks of a performative transparency model of communication. I argue that this model of communication is better suited to study transparency in action and can be applied regardless of the particular social institution that seeks to be transparent.

The emergence and solidification of transparency

It is important to remember that transparency was developed in another time, in another place, in another setting, and for another purpose than to serve as a tool to improve the credibility and accountability of an increasingly underfunded digital journalism in a fragmented public sphere. This indicates that there are probably some traits of transparency that are transferable to contemporary journalism, while others are not.

It is difficult to say in which field transparency first surfaced as a practice. In one sense, early freedom of information acts, such as the Swedish *Tryckfrihetsförordningen* [Freedom of printing law] which came into force in 1766, can be viewed as a transparency measure. The law had a large element of freedom of information provision that put pressure on the government to make information publicly available (Örnebring & Karlsson, forthcoming). Thus, rather than the government operating with secrecy as a basic principle, it gives citizens the right to access government documentation and work practices and thereby forces the government to *disclose* information. However, in most of the literature on transparency, the long history of freedom of information provision is referred to in passing, as a background to, and proto-version of, transparency. One probable reason for this is that transparency is viewed as a more active measure on behalf of the government (or other institutional actors) to lucidly *explain* its behaviour. Another possible explanation is that freedom of information provision primarily refers to governmental bodies while transparency extends to include all forms of social institutions.

Whatever the origins of transparency, it has attracted attention in many fields, such as governance, health, international relations, economics, and, later, in communication and journalism. Likewise, it is hard to say when and where transparency as such was originally implemented, but the ideas behind it were discernible in the US public debate about regulation on corporate financial disclosure enacted as early as 1933 (Fung et al., 2007). In the 1950s, transparency was an issue with regard to the Cold War and the increased secrecy of (and hence calls for transparency from) the state (Fenster, 2015). Many organizational fields have incorporated transparency since and there has been an increased intensity since the mid-1990s (Fung et al., 2007). The idea of transparency has been so successful that it permeates most contemporary organizations to the extent that, to some observers, they are primarily in the transparency business (Christensen & Cornelissen, 2015, see also Etzioni, 2010). This does not automatically mean that organizations are, or want to be, transparent but that they are concerned with, and must deal with, transparency as it has become a myth. A deep-seated, celebrated, yet unchallenged principle to which they must relate. Because, explain Meyer and Rowan (1977, p. 340), "organizations are driven to incorporate the practices and procedures defined by prevailing rationalized concepts of organizational work and institutionalized in society". Adjustment to a dominant norm such as transparency, then, increases the organization's legitimacy, resource allocation, and long-term prosperity regardless of the efficacy of the norm (see also DiMaggio & Powell, 1983).

The transparency trend has not gone unnoticed by journalism and has been embraced, at least emblematically, by media organizations. Hence, the invocation of habits, the spirit or radical adoption of transparency by professional and trade organizations as detailed in Chapter 1 is an acknowledgement of the mythical status of transparency in contemporary society at large and an important normative regime to follow. To unpack the theoretical underpinnings of transparency, however, it is necessary to go back further in history.

The philosophical roots of transparency in liberal democratic theory

The roots of transparency and its allegedly important role in relation to the public can be found in political philosophy in general and liberal democratic theory in particular. The connection between Kantian philosophy and transparency was introduced in Chapter 1 through the work of Plaisance (2007). The basic idea is that transparent communication (including journalism) takes place between two rational and autonomous actors that have a stake in the outcome of the communication and that the communication itself should be easy to understand, open, honest, and reciprocal. Other liberal thinkers, such as Bentham, Locke, Madison, Mill, Rawls, Rousseau, and Weber, have also theorized about the role of transparency in public life (Fenster, 2006; Fung et al., 2007). In an oft-cited passage, James Madison (Hunt, 1900), in 1822, stated the following on the relation between government and information: "A popular Government, without popular information, or the means of acquiring it, is but a Prologue to a Farce or a Tragedy; or, perhaps both. Knowledge will forever govern ignorance: And a people who mean to be their own Governors, must arm themselves with the power which knowledge gives".

In this classical quote it is evident that for the people to have power they must have comprehensible information about what is going on in the government. That is essentially an argument for openness (see also Fenster, 2006; Fung et al., 2007). Likewise, liberal philosopher John Stuart Mill elaborated on the need for information and public debate in his discussions on different forms of government in *Considerations on Representative Government*, where he comments on criteria for good forms of government (1861/2009, p. 135):

> As between one form of popular government and another, the advantage in this respect lies with that which most widely diffuses the exercise of public functions; on the one hand, by excluding fewest from the suffrage; on the other, by opening to all classes of private citizens, so far as is consistent with other equally important objects, the widest participation in the details of judicial and administrative business; as by jury–trial, admission to municipal offices, and, above all, by the utmost *possible publicity* and *liberty of discussion*, whereby not merely a few individuals in succession, but *the whole public*, are made, to a certain extent, *participants* in the government, and *sharers in the instruction and mental exercise* derived from it.

(Author's italics)

Like Kant, Mill points to the necessity of publicity, reciprocity, and finding a common ground in order for the public to be properly involved in representative government. The primary argument from this position is that democracy cannot work without the release and deliberation of information. There has been a long struggle towards that openness (Fung et al., 2007). For instance, in the eighteenth-century English parliament, it was difficult for reports to testify what was happening in parliament as access was limited and printers could be reprimanded for spreading what was being said and even mentioning the names of those in parliament (Chittick, 1988; Maartens, 2019; Örnebring & Karlsson, forthcoming; Thomas, 1959).

Mill also stresses the importance of the relational nature of the link between publishing information on the one hand and the public being reached by and understanding this information on the other. These are interlinked, explains Mill (1861/2009, p. 44), as "[p]ublicity, for instance, is no impediment to evil, nor stimulus to good, if the public will not look at what is done; but without publicity, how could they either check or encourage what they were not permitted to see?" Publicity is a prerequisite for an informed public, but this is not enough on its own.

These political thinkers overlap in their view on the need for government to be open and the reciprocal nature of its relationship with the governed. However, even though the purpose of a democratically elected government is to serve the public, it is also a bureaucracy. Bureaucracies are inclined towards hindering the release of information, as the famous sociologist Max Weber argues (1946, p. 233; see also Fung et al., 2007 and Rourke, 1957): "Every bureaucracy seeks to increase the superiority of the professionally informed by keeping their knowledge and intentions secret. Bureaucratic administration always tends to be an administration of 'secret session'; in so far as it can, it hides its knowledge and action from criticism".

There seems to be a built-in conflict in representative governance where the public need, and have the right, to know what is going on. Yet, bureaucratic governance, inevitable in representative democracies, will have an information advantage compared to those on the outside of the institution. Institutional insiders will also have a hard time functioning if they are to reveal what is going on all the time and may be caught up in proceduralism instead of efficient governance (Curtin & Meijer, 2006). In this context, institutional secrecy, the antithesis to transparency, is a "functional necessity" for the institution to serve the public efficiently (Rourke, 1957, p. 540). Consequently, it is unsurprising that increased demands for disclosure do not spark enthusiasm as "state officials bemoan the significantly impaired decision-making processes" due to transparency (Fenster, 2006, p. 885 see also Fredriksson & Edwards, 2019).

Thus, governmental institutions must simultaneously be open and closed to serve the public: open for inspection and accountability; closed for efficiency. What is unearthed by this conflict is the competing institutional logics of political democracy and state bureaucracy (Alford & Friedland, 1985; Thornton & Ocasio, 2008). Regardless of what institutional logic will eventually prevail, the institution rather than the public will probably have the greatest influence due to information asymmetry. Information asymmetry occurs because the governmental institution has the upper hand and the public it is serving has an information disadvantage. Governmental bureaucracies are complex and will be inclined towards secrecy as they (Fenster, 2006, p. 920) "...know what information they have produced and where such information is stored and, through that monopoly of knowledge about their own information, retain significant discretion over the existence and ultimate release of documents".

Together, the competing institutional logics and the information asymmetry generate a very sophisticated legitimacy and trust problem. The institution cannot be too open or too closed and it has an information advantage. It is here where transparency comes in and is predicted to disentangle the intricate web. By achieving visible (e.g. transparent) decision-making that the public can scrutinize if it is so inclined, the institution offers a way to be open without necessarily involving the public in every decision or every step of the decision-making process (Alt et al., 2002; Ball, 2009; Fung et al., 2007). Transparency releases the tension between the institutional logics and decreases the information asymmetry. Ball (2009, p. 301) poignantly explains the rationale behind it as follows: "[T]ransparency increases confidence in the decisions of government and elected officials by reducing asymmetries of information between political actors and voters, in turn creating a greater degree of public trust in political actors".

With this quote we are at the same time back in Chapter 1 where we started and somewhere else completely. The line of reasoning overlaps closely with how transparency is viewed in journalism, but the context in which it is applied is fundamentally different to journalism. Transparency was originally conceived to address issues in – using the language of institutional theory – the intersection of the institutional logic of state bureaucracy and political democracy, while journalism is a commercial product offered on a capitalistic market. This is not the only difference.

Comparing the transparency dimension in governmental and journalistic institutions

Transparency, as it was conceived by eighteenth- and nineteenth-century philosophers, was originally not designed for journalism at all (and that is using "designed" in a very generous way). And – a related point that we cannot dwell further upon here – the journalism that was around at the time transparency was conceived did not look like anything we would label "journalism" today (see Örnebring & Karlsson, forthcoming and Schudson, 1978, for extended accounts of how journalism has evolved). The point of departure for the purpose that transparency was originally supposed to serve is thus extremely far from the starting point of the contemporary debate, as introduced in Chapter 1, about the reinstitutionalization of high modern journalism.

To illustrate a few of the gaps that must be bridged when transferring the concept of transparency from a public accountability tool of governmental organizations to journalism, Table 2.1 below provides an overview on a number of dimensions concerning government and journalism organizations where they have different inclinations due to their respective institutional logic. Quite obviously, this is a streamlined approach and disregards overlap and hybrid organizations such as public service broadcasters. Nevertheless, as a heuristic tool it can be useful to think about the dimensions where journalistic and other institutions (in this case governmental) can diverge and what this entails for the role of transparency. For reasons of simplicity, the use of "government" from now on refers to both elected officials that can be replaced after public elections and public servants who work within various administrative capacities in public organizations (e.g. healthcare, authorities, education, etc.) that in one way or another answer to the government and, by extension, the parliament and the citizens. Throughout the book the setting in which transparency is discussed will be representative democracies where free elections are held.

Table 2.1 Some dimensions where governmental and journalistic organizations differ

Area of comparison	Governmental organizations	Journalistic organizations
Type of organization	State bureaucracy	Capitalist enterprise
Coercion on constituents	Inescapable	Easily escapable (at least individual organizations, although media as a social institution is not)
Form of organization	Complex interdependent bureaucracies	Private companies
Working rhythm	Long arc, slow and few updates	Short arc, fast and many updates
Inclination to keep information secret	High	Low

Type of organization. Government and journalistic institutions are driven by fundamentally different institutional logics (Alford & Friedland, 1985; Thornton & Ocasio, 2008). Government organizations are public organizations. They have a mandate from people whom they should serve and to whom they answer. Therefore, transparency and accountability are inscribed in these institutions. In a democracy there is no way around that.

Journalism, on the other hand, is a commercial enterprise and it does not have a formal elective mandate from its audience, although it warms to the idea of representing the public. Rhetorically, serving the public comes high on the journalistic agenda as the role of journalism is stressed as being important in providing an arena for debate and information about what is going on in government and as a watchdog if government officials try something dodgy. However, in reality, the public is more important and liked in the abstract rather than in the concrete (Breed, 1955; de Sola Pool & Shulman, 1959; Gans, 2004; Sumpter, 2000). Less celebrated but nonetheless crucial is the need to make profit and answer to stockholders. The reinstitutionalization of journalism is at least, if not more, driven by commercial as it is by normative concerns. Thus, transparency is an added value. But unless it increases the legitimacy and turnover of the media organizations it has no value and journalism can, as it did before, opt out of transparency.

Coercion on constituents. In the modern nation state there is no way of avoiding being affected by the government in a wide range of areas such as taxes, the educational system, the penal system, conscription, etc. (O'Neill, 2002). Therefore, transparency is a way of understanding and holding government accountable for its unavoidable actions. When this is provided, it is a way of building legitimacy for the institution. If unavoidability is an argument for why transparency is needed, the situation is quite different for journalism, as it is quite easy for its potential public to simply choose to surf other websites, turn off the TV set, or not buy the paper. Instead, under the capitalistic institutional logic, the demand for the product, circulation or reach is a way to build legitimacy – "look how many people voluntarily request our services". The fact that people increasingly choose not to consume news is one of the reasons, as mentioned in Chapter 1, that transparency is considered in the first place. The principal question, then, concerns the extent to which a measure such as transparency that was born out of tensions between the institutional logics of state bureaucracy and political democracy is applicable in the market. Launching the issue from the perspective of those tensions, we could ask: to what extent are perceived coercion and lack of accountability something that bothers journalism's constituents, and is "exit" a pertinent tactic?

Organizational complexity. Modern governmental administration also brings a level of organizational complexity that is not necessarily transferable to journalism (Fenster, 2015). If transparency is about explaining the decisions made by an organization, then the preconditions for the two types of institution are distinct. It is probably easier to understand and get an answer to why a particular news story was framed the way it was than it is to get an individual piece of legislation explained. In the first case, one can ask the journalist in the by-line. In the case of laws, they usually do not come with a by-line, so if one wonders about the background of a particular law one should perhaps ask...the parliament? As a result, the organizational complexity is likely to impinge on how transparency is enacted. In a complex organization, there is probably greater need for guidelines, documentation, control, audits, and other things that enable traceable decision-making (i.e. transparent decision-making). Thus, governmental transparency is likely to be rather complex and – highly likely – non-transparent. By contrast, then, transparency in less complex organizations could in its crudest form be "answer questions if there are any".

Publishing rhythms. The institutions diverge on their information publishing rhythms in two dimensions related to time. However, first it is important to make a distinction regarding the reach of the communication between the institutions. There are millions of governmental decisions made daily in regard to healthcare, admission to universities, sentences in courts, etc., but most of those decisions impact few people. Journalism is historically aimed at many people at once. Thus, most decisions (and related communication) by government are not aimed at the greater public, while this *is* the case for journalism. Since the transparency debate is largely about the relation between the institution and the public at large, the publishing rhythms of those types of communication are in focus here. The governmental institutions typically work for a *long* time to get to *few* decisions out in public, and thus the communication windows will likewise be few and far between. One medium-sized news organization alone churns out *hundreds* of items daily, and the time it takes from when a piece of information arrives at the newsroom until it is published can be measured in seconds, if not less (Örnebring & Karlsson, forthcoming; van Dalen, 2012; Wu et al., 2018). Thus, the number of items in need of transparency and the time available to allocate each of these items to transparency measures varies substantially among the institutions. Also, the role of publishing itself is rather different in these institutions. For journalistic institutions, publishing is *the* thing they are occupied with and this is typically a decentralized activity (e.g. the individual journalist and local editor do most of the work). Publishing is also *the* contact with its constituents. For governmental services, *the* contact with its constituents is probably made by low-ranking public servants. The publishing activities, on the other hand, are more likely to be centralized. Contrasting the two institutions, journalistic institutions conduct many performances every day and the actors carrying out the performances are also those best equipped to explain them. Governmental institutions, however, make few appearances every day and those who make the decisions are not necessarily present to explain them.

Inclination to secrecy. The inclination of the state bureaucracy is to keep information secret. The purpose of journalism is to publish, often the things that the state bureaucracy is trying to keep secret, thereby making the government more transparent and accountable. Publishing information is the *raison d'être* for journalism for two reasons: first, in terms of monetizing it through subscriptions and advertising; second, to utilize it for social legitimacy (e.g. providing useful information about, amongst other things, shady officials). The fact that journalism tries to keep the government transparent and accountable does not necessarily mean that journalism itself must be more transparent. If publishing information about the government is a way to accumulate economic and social capital, it must also be asked what capital can be accumulated by publishing information about journalism and to what extent journalism itself (or any other institution) is the recipient of that capital.

In summary, there are several dimensions where the social institution of journalism, at least as we currently understand it, differs from the social institution – i.e. government – that triggered the founding justifications of transparency. There are probably other dimensions that differ between the social institutions that might be worth exploring. One is that government is meticulously regulated not only by law but also guidelines, funding, and instructions while journalism prefers as little law as possible (e.g. a "free press"). Relatedly, there are vast differences in the commitment to security, safety, and responsibility to protect constituents, where governmental institutions have a high score (defence, police, healthcare, etc.), while it is low in journalism (i.e. do not harm). Another dimension is that government institutions are inhabited by elected officials and public servants while journalism hosts semi-professionals with self-defined ethics. Finally, the type of power differs, in that journalism has symbolic power while government spans several areas.

What this means for the feasibility of transparency in journalism is currently hard to say (at least for this author) but it is something that we, as researchers of journalism, need to better explore and consider.

One thing particularly worth highlighting is the inevitability of government in any organized social life and therefore the need for various ways to hold it accountable. *This* is the original rationale for transparency. Contrast this with journalism, where, if you are dissatisfied with journalism, you can just walk away. That option is utterly unobtainable with government. This means that there are different dynamics at play.

This section has highlighted some aspects of transparency that are rarely discussed in the literature. Instead, transparency has been imported into journalism without much consideration of its origin or how the public would respond to it. Some of the issues raised here will be revisited in the following chapters (mainly Chapter 5), but in my view, the issues raised here need to be explored in depth. After this exposé of differences between how transparency could serve/not serve a journalistic organization compared to others, it is time to look at the substantial overlaps between different types of organizations.

The implicit theory of transparency

Regardless of the different institutional logics that permeate organizations and what problems are supposed to be resolved by transparency, there are similarities across various fields of what comprise the core institutional problems and the solution transparency promises that builds on the suggestions made by liberal philosophers. This can tentatively be labelled "the implicit theory[1] of transparency". The crux of the argument goes something like this.

Transparency can be a useful tool when there is a perceived information asymmetry (Alt et al., 2002; Ball, 2009; Fung et al., 2007) that needs to be addressed. This can be, for instance, when the public are unaware of how a news story is put together, or what car has the best fuel economy or safety score, or the waiting time and success rate of healthcare providers in the treatment of a disease. Moreover, this information asymmetry is forecast to negatively impact the authority and legitimacy of the institution in question due to prospective mistrust among the public (e.g. "How do I *really know* that this is the best fuel economy?" etc.).

To achieve the *effect* of correcting the information asymmetry, decreasing mistrust/increasing trust, and to sustain or improve institutional authority and legitimacy, the following fundamentals are involved: *sender* (sometimes labelled "disclosures"), *message, channels*, and *receiver* (sometimes labelled "users") where the sender (or organization insider – journalist, official, public servant etc.) has an information advantage over the public/receiver/user (Fenster, 2006, 2015). To be able to serve the need of the disadvantaged, the sender needs to open up reciprocal channels of communication and learn about their expectations or alternatively educate the receiver in how X (where X is the activity in need of enlightenment) really works.

This is possible through honest communication where intentions, ideals, skills, practices, expectations, etc. can be transferred from sender to receiver and vice versa. Once a mutual and consensual understanding has been developed, the sender needs to visibly demonstrate how they perform so that the quality of their performance can be adequately evaluated by the attentive and knowledgeable receivers. Should the communicated and agreed-upon standards be violated by the senders, the receivers, or more likely advocacy groups claiming to represent receivers, can hold the institution publicly accountable. Since no institutions want that, their ways will most likely be corrected, eventually getting in line with the programme.

Several desirable effects have been accomplished. When performance and (high) expectations align, information symmetry is strengthened. Authority and legitimacy for the sender/organization follow and the user gets the performance/service that they want/need/deserve/pay for and feel that they can trust the institution. Transparency was the indispensable tool to achieve these effects.

The experienced student of communication will probably by now have identified several problematic underlying assumptions in this line of reasoning. We will return to this in greater detail later in the book (in the final two chapters). For now, it is sufficient to spell out that the communication theory underpinning transparency is linear, consensual, instrumentalist, presupposes good intention from organizations and a homogeneous audience, and largely disregards structural factors and restraints.

Law professor Mark Fenster (2006, p. 885; see also Christensen & Cheney, 2015) makes this point eloquently when commenting on the state, transparency, and the role of communication: "Transparency theory's flaws result from a simplistic model of linear communication that assumes that information, once set free from the state that creates it, will produce an informed, engaged public that will hold officials accountable". If we replace the state with the black box of news media and officials with journalists, it is, in short, the gist of the transparency theory in journalism that we familiarized ourselves with earlier in the book. If people only have journalism sufficiently explained to them, they will realize their flawed ways of the past and happily join the bandwagon. Moreover, this way of viewing people and communication departs from the needs that *journalism*, not people, has (Heim & Craft, 2020).

An oppositional theory of transparency would instead point to the fact that senders can try everything to conceal and mislead their audiences. The public might be uninterested: they are far from homogeneous and in conflict with each other and the sender. Communication is difficult and often breaks down despite good intentions. There will always be someone who is at a disadvantage in communication, and why would anyone in their right mind strive to cement consensus about that?

Regardless of this very valid critique, there are still many organizations that believe in, and work with, transparency. It is also difficult to argue that organizations should not try to be transparent due to the societal standing of the norm (Christensen & Cornelissen, 2015). Despite the objections, transparency occasionally produces some of the desired effects and receives appreciation from the public both in journalism (Curry & Stroud, 2019; Karlsson et al., 2014) and elsewhere (Fung et al., 2007). In other words, at times transparency seems to work according to its proposed function and it is necessary to chart some of the common ground of transparency across different fields.

The performative transparency model

Chapter 1 explained how both the journalistic profession and industry stressed the importance of the transparency norm and being as transparent as possible in journalistic practice. This applies irrespective of what kind of institution is in question. The theory must (appear to) touch ground and be applied in practice to be used by journalists and experienced by its audience, practised by public servants and requested by citizens, applied by healthcare personnel and intelligible to patients and their relatives. Transparency needs to move from abstract principle to "ceremonial conformity", shared by everyone involved (Christensen & Cornelissen, 2015; Meyer & Rowan, 1977). To be able to chart the practice of transparency we need to have a model that both allows it to be described in principle and empirical observations to be carried out. Additionally, the model needs to offer more than the simplistic and linear model of communication that currently permeates the debate.

For the rest of the chapter, we will leave the debate on whether transparency is effective, desirable or feasible in the first place and instead focus on the prerequisites of how different fields think about *how* to communicate transparency and/or transparently. There will be a move away from the macro to the micro level. Irrespective of whether the organization is commercial or public, there are arguably some components that are necessary if transparency is to materialize at all. It is likely that you will find them, perhaps under different synonyms, in most work dealing with how transparency is "done" within various fields. The implicit theory of transparency also harbours a linear model of communication with different parts – sender, channel, message, receiver, and effect. Although this model is crude it still identifies some building blocks that can be used in proposing a slightly more advanced model of communication that is discernible in previous research. Several texts place emphasis on the performative, reciprocal, and negotiable aspect of transparency, thus indicating those components as particularly important in a transparency communication model.

Plaisance (2007, p. 188) writes in his definition that "...transparent behavior can be defined as *conduct* [author's italics] that presumes an openness in communication and serves a reasonable expectation of forthright exchange when parties have a legitimate stake in the possible outcomes or effects of the communicative act". Thus, Plaisance's definition implies that transparency is indeed a performance, although he uses the words "behaviour" and "conduct", but they also refer to an act that is displayed to others. Similarly, the European Union writes in the European Union Law Treaty establishing a Constitution for Europe, Part I, Title VI – The Democratic Life of the Union, Article I-50 on the transparency of the proceedings of the Union, bodies, offices and agencies, that "[i]n order to promote good governance and ensure the participation of civil society, the Union institutions, bodies, offices and agencies shall conduct their work as openly as possible". Here too there is a conduct that should be open. Ball (2009; see also Fenster, 2006) approaches transparency through metaphors, and she indicates that the role of these metaphors is to explain how organizations and states should openly conduct their daily decision-making. More specifically, she writes (p. 299) that "[t]ransparency is a series of actions creating credible governance systems, visible performance measurement systems...". Transparency is a visible performance that should be in the open, not mere information to be sent from A to B.

The nomenclature used quite closely aligns with Goffman's theory of social interaction and dramaturgical approaches to role performance (Goffman, 2004). Goffman suggests that people are actors who move upon a stage to deliver a performance that is intended to make a desired impression on an audience. To put on the best performance, they will bring some things to the frontstage while other things will be kept backstage. Transparency is likewise about impression management. It is about delivering a performance in the open with the intention of making previous hidden practices or information visible, moving them from the backstage to the frontstage, opening up the black box that purportedly is the problem with the expectation that increased trust will ensue (Karlsson, 2011).

In that spirit, I suggest that what can be tentatively called the "Performative Transparency Model" (henceforth PTM), detailed at length below, is a useful approach to studying how transparency is enacted. When transparency becomes a part of journalistic role performance, this ties together the norms with the daily practice (Karlsson & Clerwall, 2019; Mellado, 2015). Using the framework of institutional theory (Thornton & Ocasio, 2008; Vos, 2020), the institutions are, amongst other things, constituted by routinized practices. Synthesizing this view with Goffman's notion of performance and the idea that transparency is carried out in the open, we can understand transparent performances as routinized institutional practices that are conducted in front of the public.

Another argument as to why "performance" is a fitting word is the character of digital media where, technically, everything is accessible at the same time but very few things are highly visible. One dimension of digital media is that there is a continuing stream of published news items that get only a short time in the limelight, meaning that things pass over the stage at a high speed. Second, while the publishing speed is high the archives are always accessible, meaning that any old and "spent" news item can be pulled out from the backstage and put under the spotlight at any time. Third, the shelf time and returning power of news stories are tangential upon the attention they receive from the public – how the performance is received. In short, the performance metaphor fits well with the properties of digital media.

The building blocks of the model are stage, actors, script, aesthetics and delivery, and finally effects. Whatever else can be taken away from transparent forms of communication, as they are currently perceived, these must remain, otherwise the tools or techniques used to achieve the goals of transparency will be severely hampered or even implode, and the performance will not deliver.

The key difference between the implicit theory of transparency and the performative transparency model is that the model details how transparency is enacted while the implicit theory forecasts the consequences of that enactment. Thus, it is possible to enact transparently according to the model with the outcome, without any tangible outcome, or with the opposite outcome that the implicit theory suggests.

Stage

For transparency to occur, it needs to be harboured somewhere, to take *place*. We can label this a "setting", a "medium of communication", a "window", a "stage", or something else. I will use the stage metaphor as it connects well to communication as performance grounded in

Goffman's theory of social interaction. The word "stage" also makes it evident that not all things will be brought "on stage", or "frontstage" to use Goffman's term, but may remain hidden or "backstage" and thus non-transparent even as previously unseen things are moved onstage. Thus, being more transparent than before does not mean being completely transparent, and some things that used to be on the stage can be moved backstage. The important characteristics of the stage are that it is durable in time, spreadable in space, and allows reciprocity. The time dimension is important because otherwise it will be impossible to compare current with previous behaviour and statements, and thus evaluate any standards. The spreadability in space is crucial, especially for organizations with large audiences, as it is otherwise impossible for a wide variety and large number of users to learn about, express preference for, and evaluate the transparency measures taken. Reciprocity is needed since transparency is essentially about "forthright exchange" concerning expectations and evaluations of the public, and unless there is some form of reciprocity the sender cannot know about them. The higher the score in these dimensions, the better the stage can fulfil its purpose of accommodating transparency. The stage needs to be hosted "somewhere". This can be, for example, on a news website or on a social media platform. It is likely that different stages foster different expectations of transparency as different media are permeated by different logics that influence what is published (Strömbäck, 2008; van Dijck & Poell, 2013). What can be said on Twitter might not be suitable for a news site; what is suitable for a news site might be too stiff for Twitter. There can be one or several stages in which transparency concurrently takes place.

Actors: Journalists and the public

With a stage in place, actors can populate it. The transparency stage involves as a bare minimum two actors, journalists (disclosures/senders) and the public (receivers/users), and their relationships. It is important to keep in mind that regulators, critics, advertisers, peers, etc. are also constituents with a stake in transparency, possibly with conflicting views, but the focus is mainly on journalists and the public. They are the key recipients and stakeholders of transparency, and most transparency debate gravitates around this relationship and how to improve the trust. One set of actors, journalists, will have a greater job to do, but both have important roles to play. Journalists are the ones who ostensibly are to conduct journalism more transparently through various measures. They are the insiders on the advantageous side of information asymmetry and are thus able to explain and make their performance more open. They will occupy most, if not all, of the stage. Some journalistic actors will be more enthused than others. The public have a less active but still crucial role, as transparency, or any other norm, will not work without public approval (Schudson, 2001). Someone needs to applaud and boo at the right places, so the cast know that the play was alright, or alternatively change how the play is enacted. The input from the public should have an impact on how the journalistic actors perform, but the input cannot dictate the journalistic performance, because that would negate journalism's autonomy and professionalism. The purpose of transparency is about rehabilitating journalism through increased trust, not abolishing it to please the public.

Script

The stage is set, and the actors have arrived; another crucial component is to decide what transparency is and how it should be performed. Regardless of conflicting desires and the problems of reaching a mutual understanding, there needs to be a common ground and shared views of what constitutes a transparent and non-transparent performance – a *script* for the journalists to follow and the public to evaluate. This common ground can only be accomplished if it is durable over time and spreadable in space. The transparency script cannot only concern a few present people but citizens at large out of sight and time with each other for at least two reasons. First, journalism is by definition a public concern, otherwise the issues it seeks to address could be handled in a member's club. Second, a transparent act must be similar regardless of what stage it is performed on, or by what actors, otherwise it will neither be an institution-wide norm and practice nor allow the audience to gauge the extent to which the promised and expected path of performance is followed.

The script needs to have guidelines that are detailed enough to direct the performance of individual journalists so that they know what a transparent act is. Moreover, the script needs to be tied to journalistic skills and routines, as this is where transparency is supposed to "happen" and connect actual journalistic performance with the transparency norm. If journalists are not in possession of transparency skills, they need to be trained in them as they would otherwise be unable to perform their work transparently. Such skills and routines can, for example, include, but not be limited to, acknowledging mistakes and making corrections, explaining the news selection and framing process, providing hyperlinks, addressing reader feedback, being called out to declare and defend their position on a sensitive issue that they are covering, and much more. Much previous research has been engaged with this line of inquiry, what journalists are doing to be transparent and what they think of it.

Setting aside the fact that members of the public will probably have diverging (if any) wishes in terms of what journalists should deliver, journalism has many different organizational layers. In what areas and aspects of the journalistic performance is transparency more crucial compared to others? It can range from ownership and the preferences of the owners to the preferences of individual journalists (furthermore, in what areas and where should the line be drawn? If political leaning is to be posted, what about membership in organizations, income, sexuality, recently borrowed books at the library, etc.). It can concern how and why news is selected, collected, processed, assembled, distributed, updated, and commented or not commented upon, among many other issues.

The aesthetics and delivery of transparency

By now we have established a stage on which transparency can be performed. We have identified a few key actors – journalists and the public. The actors have deliberated on what areas of journalism should be transparent. Journalists have proposed what they should do to be transparent, and the public have given their feedback with regard to what they expect journalists to do to be transparent. In addition to these components, we also need to add how transparency is delivered. Just because something is in the script it does not follow that it is presented with ingenuity or clarity. Transparency measures need to be translated into language, signs, symbols, and design elements that are easy to get across to a public that are diverse in terms of interest, opportunity, ability, and demographics.

Ball (2009, p. 300 see also Grimmelikhuijsen, 2012) draws attention to this issue in her review of transparency in different fields and says that transparency programmes must deliver "understandable, usable, quality information to the public on inputs, outputs, and outcomes". Information asymmetry is not addressed by simply making information available if no one notices, understands, or acts upon it. The transparency measures should be desirable and understandable to the public while not violating or putting too high demands on journalistic skills, practices, norms, and ideals. In other words, for transparency to have a chance to work it needs to be manifested in, or in the vicinity of, journalistic content that is intelligible and fit for use by journalists as well as the public. Just as Barnhurst and Nerone (2001) argue about the importance of the *form of news* for journalism generally, there is an inescapable *form* dimension of transparency.

An example can perhaps serve to illustrate this. Accuracy is a key virtue in journalism for journalists and the audience alike. Unfortunately, errors will happen and need to be dealt with as they are a breach of journalistic professionalism, and the public deem errors and corrections important to primarily avoid, but when they occur, they should be acknowledged and admitted. A transparent way of dealing with errors would be in the line of "admit when errors have been made and correct them". Indeed...but in what form, what level of detail, when, where, under what circumstances and by whom should this be done? It could be in the form of a policy document explaining the general guidelines. It could be a sticker saying "News not yet finalized, be wary of errors". It could be a detailed explanation of the error, what caused the error and the corrected version of the news together with the incorrect version. Yet, all of these are in some way or other "corrections" and thus transparent.

Corrections are typically, at least in the author's native country of Sweden, published in a short and decontextualized form in a dedicated column in the newspaper a day or longer after the initial publishing of the erroneous news report. Silverman (2014, p. 154) argues that there are two problems with corrections. The first is that there are too few of them in relation to how many errors are made (Maier, 2007), and the second that they "...are often written to minimize the damage of the error, rather than communicate the correct information and express regret for the mistake". We know little about which is the most desirable or effective way of communicating errors and corrections. What is probably the most convenient way for the news organization to communicate might not help bring the maximum transparency effect. There are innumerable ways to communicate transparency, but so far few have been tested or researched. We know little about what is considered a comprehensible and visually appealing transparent performance by the public.

Effect

In Goffman's view, a performance is enacted to leave a certain impression on an audience. But it is up to the audience to decide whether it is convinced or not. Should it not be convinced, the performance has failed and needs to be revised. The same can be applied to transparency. If a transparent performance does not have the desired effect (e.g. positive impact on trust), it does not work as intended, because, as Ball (2009; see also Christensen & Cheney, 2015) stresses, transparency is ultimately about having some sort of effect that would otherwise be absent. Using education as an example, she writes (Ball, 2009, p. 300):

A transparent policy is deemed effective when the public acts on the information the policy provides. If an education agency provides information on the quality of schools through performance measurement, and parents choose their child's school based upon this information, the policy is said to be effective. Transparency, then, relates to inputs, outputs, and outcomes of decisions.

Transparency is indeed related to inputs and outputs, as detailed above, but also *outcomes*. In the literature there is a leaning towards the notion that transparency should *change* or *improve* things (e.g. increase public trust in the institution). But effects can also be about maintaining the status quo and preventing drastic changes such as keeping the high trust or softening the blow in the face of a likely crisis. These kinds of effects are more challenging to measure. Nevertheless, for transparency to have any legitimacy or place in journalism, it needs to have some effect, to make some difference. If not, both journalists and the public will be equally well (or poorly) off with as without it. Furthermore, transparency must influence the *public*. A foundation for transparency is that it is a tool that should improve the relationship with the public. It is perfectly fine if it serves other actors too, but it *must* impact on the public. Therefore, it is vital to empirically explore the effects of transparency on the public. What elements of the public are cheering or booing the performance? Is the cheering louder than the boos? What is the noise level? Is anyone reacting at all? Is the noise level co-dependent on other dimensions?

Absent effects are thus problematic and can be for several possible reasons. The basic idea of transparency is correct, but either the script (what it is in practice) or the delivery (how it is dressed up) is off. It may be the wrong actors on stage, or the stage may be wrong. Alternatively, the idea that a transparent performance will deliver the desired effect is based on flawed assumptions.

Unless a multitude of scenarios are empirically explored, we will know little of the actual effects of transparency. Chapter 3 presents a review of empirical studies that has been conducted thus far, while Chapter 5 raises some principal concerns about why the desired effect might be hard to accomplish.

Black box and glass box

The performative transparency model identifies several interlinked components that need to be in place for transparency to occur and offers a way to study transparency *in practice*. The performance can be more or less transparent or not transparent at all. More things can be moved from backstage to the frontstage and thus become a part of the now transparent performance, or they can remain hidden. If we reuse the metaphor that non-transparent journalism is a black box, then a very transparent journalism would be a glass box, where most of the things that went on inside it would be visible and graspable to those on the outside. The glass box would also be permeable enough to allow communication to flow between the inside and outside. We could even imagine a scale where the "black box" is at one end and the "glass box" at the other, with various degrees of opacity/transparency between them. However, the glass box would still need to have boundaries to demarcate what is inside and outside, and thus who would be responsible and accountable for what comes out of it, or else it would be an "air box", which would not be a box at all.

If the transparency measures could be made detailed enough, there could be ranks, scores, levels, badges, and the like. Regardless of whether that kind of exercise would be interesting or conceivable, the basic premise behind transparency rests on the same idea – that there is a way to meaningfully separate a transparent from a non-transparent performance. In doing so, it is also implied that this can be accomplished at a detailed level – much like, I would argue, the way it is outlined above.

Summary

This chapter has looked at the philosophical roots of transparency. It has further detailed how transparency has been viewed by other social institutions and some of the differences and overlaps there are between them and journalism. It has argued that there is a fundamental difference between the two fields and that some aspects of transparency might not be transferable to journalism. But the case has also been made that, through the introduction of the implicit theory of transparency and the performative transparency model of communication, there are some components that are identical across institutions. The first two chapters have been committed to discussing transparency both in principle and theoretically. Chapter 3, coming up next, assesses the reality of transparency as it has been implemented and evaluated thus far.

Note

1 I am indebted to Fenster, who uses transparency theory (2006, 2015) and the linear model (2015) to describe the same phenomenon. However, I choose to use the term "implicit theory" because the literature rarely

discusses any theory of transparency, or components thereof, explicitly. Nevertheless, when the argument is laid bare, a rather distinct theoretical proposition emanates.

References

Alford, R., & Friedland, R. (1985). *Powers of Theory: Capitalism, the State and Democracy.* Cambridge University Press. https://doi.org/10.1086/228660.

Alt, J. E., Lassen, D. D., & Skilling, D. (2002). Fiscal transparency, gubernatorial approval, and the scale of government: Evidence from the states. *State Politics and Policy Quarterly,* 2(3), 230–250.

Ball, C. (2009). What is transparency? *Public Integrity,* 11(4), 293–308. https://doi.org/10.2753/PIN1099-9922110400.

Barnhurst, K. G., & Nerone, J. C. (2001). *The Form of News.* The Guilford Press.

Breed, W. (1955). Social control in the newsroom: A functional analysis. *Social Forces,* 33(4), 326–335. www.jstor.org/stable/10.2307/2573002.

Chittick, K. (1988). Dickens and parliamentary reporting in the 1830s. *Victorian Periodicals Review,* 21(4), 151–160.

Christensen, L. T., & Cheney, G. (2015). Peering into transparency: Challenging ideals, proxies, and organizational practices. *Communication Theory,* 25(1), 70–90. https://doi.org/10.1111/comt.12052.

Christensen, L. T., & Cornelissen, J. (2015). Organizational transparency as myth and metaphor. *European Journal of Social Theory,* 18(2), 132–149. https://doi.org/10.1177/1368431014555256.

Curry, A. L., & Stroud, N. J. (2019). The effects of journalistic transparency on credibility assessments and engagement intentions. *Journalism.* https://doi.org/10.1177/1464884919850387.

Curtin, D., & Meijer, A. J. (2006). Does transparency strengthen legitimacy? A critical analysis of European Union policy documents. *Information Polity,* 11(2), 109–122.

de Sola Pool, I., & Shulman, I. (1959). Newsmen' s fantasies, audiences, and newswriting. *The Public Opinion Quarterly,* 23(2), 145–158.

DiMaggio, P. J., & Powell, W. W. (1983). The iron cage revisited: Institutional isomorphism and collective rationality in organizational fields. *American Sociological Review,* 48(2), 147–160.

Etzioni, A. (2010). Is transparency the best disinfectant? *Journal of Political Philosophy,* 18(4), 389–404. https://doi.org/10.1111/j.1467-9760.2010.00366.x.

Fenster, M. (2006). The opacity of transparency. *Iowa Law Review,* 91(3), 885–949.

Fenster, M. (2015). Transparency in search of a theory. *European Journal of Social Theory,* 18(2), 150–167. https://doi.org/10.1177/1368431014555257.

Fredriksson, M., & Edwards, L. (2019). Communicating under the regimes of divergent ideas: How public agencies in Sweden manage tensions between transparency and consistency. *Management Communication Quarterly,* 33(4), 548–580. https://doi.org/10.1177/0893318919859478.

Fung, A., Graham, M., & Weil, D. (2007). *Full Disclosure: The Perils and Promise of Transparency*. Cambridge University Press. https://doi.org/10.1111/j.1747-1346.2008.00128.x.

Gans, H. (2004). *Deciding What's News*. Illinois University Press.

Goffman, E. (2004). *Jaget och maskerna: En studie i vardagslivets dramatik*. Norstedts.

Grimmelikhuijsen, S. (2012). Linking transparency, knowledge and citizen trust in government: An experiment. *International Review of Administrative Sciences*, 78(1), 50–73. https://doi.org/10.1177/0020852311429667.

Heim, K., & Craft, S. (2020). Transparency in journalism: Meanings, merits, and risks. In L. Wilkins & C. Christians (Eds.), *The Routledge Handbook of Mass Media Ethics* (pp. 308–320). Routledge.

Hunt, G. (1900). *The Writings of James Madison*. G.P. Putnam's Sons.

Karlsson, M. (2011). The immediacy of online news, the visibility of journalistic processes and a restructuring of journalistic authority. *Journalism*, 12(3), 279–295. https://doi.org/10.1177/1464884910388223.

Karlsson, M., & Clerwall, C. (2019). Cornerstones in journalism: According to citizens. *Journalism Studies*, 20(8), 1184–1199. https://doi.org/10.1080/1461670X.2018.1499436.

Karlsson, M., Clerwall, C., & Nord, L. (2014). You ain't seen nothing yet: Transparency's (lack of) effect on source and message credibility. *Journalism Studies*, 15(5), 668–678. https://doi.org/10.1080/1461670X.2014.886837.

Maartens, B. (2019). "What the country wanted": The houses of parliament, the press and the origins of media management in Britain 1780–1900. *Public Relations Review*, 45(2), 227–235. https://doi.org/10.1016/j.pubrev.2018.03.005.

Maier, S. R. (2007). Setting the record straight. *Journalism Practice*, 1(1), 33–43. https://doi.org/10.1080/17512780601078845.

Mellado, C. (2015). Professional roles in news content: Six dimensions of journalistic role performance. *Journalism Studies*, 16(4), 596–614. https://doi.org/10.1080/1461670X.2014.922276.

Meyer, J. W., & Rowan, B. (1977). Institutionalized organizations: Formal structure as myth and ceremony. *American Journal of Sociology*, 83(2), 340–363.

Mill, J. S. (1861/2009). *Considerations on Representative Government*. The Floating Press. https://doi.org/10.1037/12186-000.

O'Neill, O. (2002). *A Question of Trust: The BBC Reith Lectures 2002*. Cambridge University Press.

Örnebring, H. (2019). Journalism cannot solve journalism's problems. *Journalism*, 20(1), 226–228. https://doi.org/10.1177/1464884918808690.

Örnebring, H., & Karlsson, M. (forthcoming). *Journalistic Autonomy: A Genealogy of a Concept*.

Plaisance, P. L. (2007). Transparency: An assessment of the Kantian roots of a key element in media ethics practice. *Journal of Mass Media Ethics*, 22(2–3), 187–207. https://doi.org/10.1080/08900520701315855.

Rourke, F. E. (1957). Secrecy in American bureaucracy. *Political Science Quarterly*, 72(4), 540–564.

Schudson, M. (1978). *Discovering the News.* Basic Books.
Schudson, M. (2001). The objectivity norm in American journalism. *Journalism Studies*, 2(2), 149–170.
Silverman, C. (2014). Corrections and ethics: Greater accuracy through honesty. In K. McBride & T. Rosenstiel (Eds.), *The New Ethics of Journalism: Principles for the 21st Century* (pp. 151–161). Sage.
Strömbäck, J. (2008). Four phases of mediatization: An analysis of the mediatization of politics. *International Journal of Press/Politics*, 13(3), 228–246. https://doi.org/10.1177/1940161208319097.
Sumpter, R. (2000). Daily newspaper editors' audience construction routines: A case study. *Critical Studies in Media Communication*, 17(3), 334–346. https://doi.org/10.1080/15295030009388399.
Thomas, P. (1959). The beginning of parliamentary reporting in newspapers, 1768–1774. *English Historical Review*, LXXIV(293), 623–636.
Thornton, P. H., & Ocasio, W. (2008). Institutional logics. In R. Greenwood, C. Oliver, R. Suddaby & K. Sahlin (Eds.), *The SAGE Handbook of Organizational Institutionalism* (pp. 99–128). Sage. https://doi.org/10.4135/9781849200387.n4.
van Dalen, A. (2012). The algorithms behind the headlines. *Journalism Practice*, 6(5–6), 648–658. https://doi.org/10.1080/17512786.2012.667268.
van Dijck, J., & Poell, T. (2013). Understanding social media logic. *Media and Communication*, 1(1), 2–14. https://doi.org/10.1177/1745691612459060.
Vos, T. (2020). Journalism as institution. In H. Örnebring (Ed.), *The Oxford Encyclopedia of Journalism Studies* (pp. 736–750). Oxford University Press.
Weber, M. (1946). *Essays in Sociology.* Oxford University Press.
Wu, S., Tandoc, E. C., & Salmon, C. T. (2018). Journalism reconfigured: Assessing human–machine relations and the autonomous power of automation in news production. *Journalism Studies.* https://doi.org/10.1080/1461670X.2018.1521299.

3 Can you see the sunlight? Transparency at work

Chapter 1 argued that some prominent parts of journalistic institutions are vested in transparency and its future role. Chapter 2 reviewed the philosophical roots of transparency, offered some views on how transparency has been implemented, and proposed a theory of how transparency is generally understood, and a communication model to help assess transparency at work.

Although the proposition of the implicit theory of transparency is appealing and rewarding to all involved, a great deal of work is still required for it to happen. For journalists, transparency is challenging to incorporate in already existing and proven skills, practices, and routines. They must also make sure to explain both their work and the transparent ways in which they make their work accessible to the public. The public, for their part, need to pay attention to journalistic work, and possess or attain the necessary skills to comprehend it, and its transparency. Chapter 3 provides some examples of transparency from journalistic practices, as well as offering a review of the empirical evidence to date concerning how transparency has affected the everyday life of journalists, journalistic content, and the public who consume news.

The review is organized into three sections, focused on journalistic actors, content, and the public. The section on journalistic actors refers to research that, in one way or the other, studies the way that journalists and media organizations relate to transparency. The second section reviews studies investigating how transparency has been applied in relation to journalistic content. The news content is of particular interest, since it involves the stage, aesthetic, and delivery elements of the performative transparency model (PTM). The third section assesses research into the public's perspectives of transparency. The chapter ends with a discussion about the extent to which the findings support the implicit theory of transparency, and proposes some future research.

DOI: 10.4324/9780429340642-3

Before continuing, two caveats are required. First, throughout the chapter I will mostly write about journalists and journalism as one entity, although there are vast differences and inequalities between both journalistic outlets and the journalists working in them (Örnebring et al., 2018). I do this because all expressions of journalism and journalists, beyond their differences, belong to the same institution and are thus affected by the transparency issue. Second, the empirical research on transparency is, after a slow start, growing rapidly. This is also true of public debate, and thus awareness, about transparency, as exemplified by the commitment offered by professional organizations and industry leaders, described in Chapter 1. Much of the data that the research was based on was collected either before, or at the dawn of this seeming surge of transparency. Norms change, and under certain conditions some norms can change faster than others. This means that something that was almost invisible before an institutional change can be found in abundance just a decade or two later. For instance, the objectivity norm would be hard to identify in the early twentieth century, before the formation of organizations such as the American Society of News Editors (ASNE) and the SPJ, which formulated their codes of ethics, setting standards to follow, in 1922 and 1926, respectively. After these institutional milestones were set, objectivity should have been increasingly more discernible until it reached its peak some 50 or 60 years after the objectivity standards was first penned. It is possible, although in my view improbable, that future research will provide a different picture than the somewhat gloomy overview that is offered here.

Can you see the sunlight?

A recurring metaphor for the function of transparency, and a good contender with the "sausage" metaphor, is that of sunlight. The metaphor is attributed to the founder of public interest law, and later Supreme Court Justice, Louis Brandeis, who over a hundred years ago stated "[p]ublicity is justly commended as a remedy for social and industrial diseases, sunshine is said to be the best disinfectant, electric light the best policeman" (1913; cited in Fox, 2007, p. 664, but see also, amongst others, Fung et al., 2007; Williams & Delli Carpini, 2011). This is a strong metaphor that is intuitively easy to understand. If only the dark places were open and sunlight could reach them, then the mould, odour, and decay that has been allowed to grow in them would be exposed, vaporized, and replaced with light and fresh air, whether this involves the "black box" of the newsroom, complex state bureaucracies, or shady financial dealings by offshore banks.

The metaphor also reveals the distinct epistemology of communication. Letting the sunlight in, or making things visible, is in itself enough to make people aware of the problem, and thereby increase knowledge about an institution's potential wrongdoing, which will ultimately hinder corrupt behaviour (Christensen & Cornelissen, 2015; Etzioni, 2010; Fenster, 2006; Grimmelikhuijsen, 2012). It is as easy as 1–2–3: open box, let sunlight in, germs gone. In other words, the metaphor is an instantiation of the implicit theory of transparency and its linear view of communication.

Powerful as the metaphor[1] is, it remains unclear what the box, sunlight, and germs are, and how the process works in detail. For sunlight to be seen it needs to exist in the first place. That is, for transparency to be seen, it must be enacted in practice. Furthermore, one person's sunlight can be someone else's full moon or pitch darkness. If the sunlight is not seen as such, it will not accomplish the cleansing. Using the dominant metaphor of transparency as sunlight shining so brightly that it will prevent misdeeds, the overarching question for journalists and the public alike is – can you see the sunlight?

Journalistic actors

The actors with the biggest responsibility for, and importance in, the implementation of transparency are journalists. Without their consent or commitment to transparency, and their craftsmanship in making the news clear and comprehensive, there will not be any transparency at all. Remember that the principal problem that transparency is supposed to solve is information asymmetry. Journalists are the information workers undeniably best positioned to address information asymmetry in news production.

Some journalists and journalistic organizations seem to have accepted the recommendations for transparency from the SPJ, RTDNA, and Knight Commission on Trust, Media and Democracy as detailed in Chapter 1. The NiemanLab publish annual predictions from journalists and media insiders for the year to come. In the prediction for 2017, Sean Sullivan, a statehouse reporter for *NJ.com* and *The Star-Ledger*, answered his own questions "How do you serve a public that doesn't trust you anymore?" by arguing for more transparency and the need to show how the journalistic work gets done (Sullivan, 2016). For 2018, Raney Aronson-Rath, an executive producer for the PBS documentary series *Frontline*, wrote that transparency is the antidote to fake news and an important way to deepen public trust in journalism (Aronson-Rath, 2017). She explained how they worked actively with transparency through, for instance, publishing navigable transcripts. She was joined by Carrie Brown-Smith, Director of the social journalism program at the CUNY Graduate School of Journalism, and Michelle Garcia, Race and Identities Senior Editor at *Vox*, predicting that transparency would finally take off, and show how the sausage was made (Brown-Smith, 2017; Garcia, 2017). In the 2019 forecast, Nickolas Jackson, the editor-in-chief of *Pacific Standard*, argued that readers are paying attention to journalism and challenging the decisions made in the newsroom and that transparency is a way to meet these challenges (Jackson, 2018). Similarly, Kourtney Bitterly, research lead for product and design discovery at *The New York Times*, argued in her prediction for 2020 that transparency is an expectation, and that people want the curtain to be withdrawn (Bitterly, 2019). PBS co-host of the *Retro Report*, Celeste Headlee, noted in her 2021 entry "The rise of radical newsroom transparency", that "Journalists have lost patience with the lack of transparency and accountability within their leadership ranks" and suggested that radical transparency would increase in the newsroom, driven by staff, and especially among the younger cohort (Headlee, 2020). The transparency in question here involves hiring and promotion decisions, which she suggests are tainted by issues of inequity, racism, and sexism. These issues have been raised time and again in journalism, and acknowledged by journalism research, so it is no surprise that journalists are fed up with them. However, this issue is also proposed as of significant interest to the public: "Going forward, executives must be prepared to justify hiring and promotion decisions not only to staff but to the broader public". In this view, the public is not only interested in how specific news items are made, but implicitly in the larger sociological issue of what shapes the news. NiemanLab publish new predictions every year and transparency is repeatedly touted as a remedy to problems within journalism.

The *Newsroom Transparency Tracker*,[2] a joint project between *Pen America*[3] and *The Trust Project*,[4] keeps track of, and publishes, the transparency standards of several newsrooms. The tracker spans four areas, with a total of 14 variables, including corrections policy, reporter bios, and diverse staffing reports. Detailing why the project was developed, they explain that "Today, newsroom transparency is more important than ever; it can help increase trust among sceptical news consumers while empowering audiences to more deeply scrutinize the sources of information they encounter online", thus echoing and reinforcing the implicit theory of transparency.

Newsguard[5] is a similar initiative, sporting the subtitle "The Internet Trust Tool", which rates the credibility and transparency of news websites around the world. By their own account they rate over 6,000 news websites, which account for 95 per cent of online engagement with news: a substantial reach. They base their ratings on nine different criteria, including correcting and clarifying errors, clearly labelling advertising, and distinguishing between opinion and news reports. *Newsguard* charges US$2.95 a month for this service.

These examples, from sanguine views of a possible change in newsroom culture to those of commercial business, are anecdotal iterations suggesting that members of the journalistic institution are not only dedicated to transparency, but that it is also possible to develop a for-profit business based on the role of transparency in journalism. Their statements suggest that they also share the assumption that transparency is something that journalists are doing, or should be doing, and that the public (and other stakeholders) want to know the inner workings of journalism. In other words, they align with the professional organizations and industry leaders mentioned in Chapter 1 and, with that, the implicit theory of transparency.

The impression from scholarship that has investigated how journalists view and work with transparency is less clear cut. An early study[6] by Hellmueller et al. (2013) remarked that there was some support for transparency practices, and that older and more experienced women were the most supportive, indicating that transparency will not be spread evenly among journalists. Two studies, in the US (Chadha & Koliska, 2015) and Germany (Koliska & Chadha, 2018), observed that transparency was not being particularly embraced by journalists, and that the way it is implemented is more about appearing transparent than actually changing how journalism is conducted. In this sense, transparency is a nuisance that must be dealt with strategically rather than something to be integrated into the practice of journalism. This might be an example of the observation (Christensen & Cornelissen, 2015) that transparency has reached mythical standing in contemporary society, and that all business must somehow address it, regardless of whether they are simply paying lip-service or their hearts are in it.

In contrast, a recent US study using a representative survey observed that transparency seemed to have been embraced by journalists (Vu & Saldaña, 2021). The study suggests that journalists have appropriated transparency measures (e.g. limiting the use of anonymous sources, making it clear where information comes from, etc.). This was especially true among journalists who saw fake news as a threat. Transparency can thus be interpreted as a way to respond to misinformation and the discourse of fake news.

Revers (2014) undertook an extensive ethnographic study with a particular eye on Twitter, which he views as a carrier of the transparency ethic. Studying Twitter practices as expressions of transparency, he noted tensions between professional control and transparency, and that there were various approaches among the journalistic corps. Younger journalists were more inclined to welcome Twitter and transparency than older journalists. Overall, there seemed to be pressure from media companies to use Twitter for promotional and transparency reasons. The journalists saw promotional benefits too, especially younger journalists who saw Twitter as a tool to build a following that could be used to advance their careers. The fact that they used Twitter in their professional capacity impinged greatly on how they presented themselves on the platform, showing an awareness that they were effectively on a stage and that their performance had to be calculated, as it was assessed by peers and other actors. This assessment and attention were felt more strongly by journalists from national elite media than their counterparts from regional media, who likely had more freedom of action. Moreover, some journalists noted the principal difference that they could tweet more freely on their individual accounts, but were more restricted on that of their news company. In other words, the performance of transparency was very much dependent on the stage, the actors, and, presumably, the public in question.

Content: Stage, aesthetics, and delivery

If, as argued in Chapter 2, transparency must be performed (e.g. visible) on a stage (e.g. a place) then we need to know more about how news organizations accomplish this (or not), otherwise, it would be impossible to see the extent to which the news media are opening up the black box and showing "how the sausage is made", to paraphrase Singer (2005). Furthermore, unless transparency is performed visibly as regards news stories there is no chance of a transparency effect, because without transparency really touching ground in day-to-day journalism it does not matter how much it is hailed in white papers or deliberated in symposiums. Metaphorically, investigating the extent to which transparency is practiced demands investigating how much sunlight there is. This is where transparency is manifested. It is a performance according to a script, delivered on a stage where journalists and the public gather. This is arguably one of, if not the, most important areas to study.

Unfortunately, this importance is not reflected when taking stock of the collective endeavours of previous research, although there are exceptions. There are quite a few studies that specifically investigate transparency on Twitter. Lasorsa (2012) observed that journalists engaged in transparency practices on Twitter that they were highly unlikely to perform in news stories on other media. Thus, just like in the Revers (2014) article, there are some stages where a transparent performance is more suitable than others. The study also found that journalists in the national elite media were less inclined to perform transparency than their colleagues in lower-status media (an observation also confirmed by Revers, 2014). In another article ostensibly based on the same dataset, Lasorsa (2012) compared the gendered practice of transparency and found that, in parallel to the survey study by Hellmueller et al. (2013), women were most likely to embrace transparency. In a study on Swedish journalists, Hedman (2016) reports that a quarter of journalist tweets are explicitly transparent, and that disclosure transparency is the preferred form.

Evidently, Twitter has been assigned particular weight in relation to transparency by academics, according to the relatively large number of studies, and has been seen "as a carrier of the ethic of transparency" (Revers, 2014, p. 823). While Twitter is certainly *a* carrier it is unlikely that it is *the* carrier of the transparency ethic, or even an important carrier. If transparency is a tool with which to mend broken relationships between the media and the public, the Twitter "stage" does not extend far enough to reach most people. Instead, Twitter transparency is a performance played out in front of a small and unrepresentative elite public, consisting of primarily peers, politicians, and academics. It is the stage that has the greatest reach and cultural relevance that will be *the* carrier of the transparency ethic. At present this is arguably still the news websites, whether reached directly or via other platforms such as search engines or referrals from social networking sites.

There have, however, been few studies of news sites or actual news stories. One early exception is Rupar (2006) who undertook a case study of transparent news gathering processes in New Zealand, and found them lacking. To the best of my knowledge there is currently only one study (Karlsson, 2010) that has attempted a systematic analysis of the extent to which different transparency techniques are used in everyday journalism. The study compared the front pages of major legacy news outlets in Sweden, the UK, and the US over one week, and found that the use of transparency was only slightly more than embryonic. Slightly different patterns of implementation were also noted, suggesting that cultural context might be important. However, the study was more than a decade ago and can hardly be relied on to say anything about transparency practices today. Follow-up studies are badly overdue, and should, if the theoretical prediction is right, show that transparency is more common nowadays.

Both news content and journalists are on the same side in the transparency relationship – the production side. Based on the, admittedly limited, evidence so far, a reasonable conclusion is that transparent performances exist, but are limited. Furthermore, different actors – elite vs non-elite, newcomers vs veterans, men vs women – relate differently to transparency. The cultural context (e.g. countries), as well as the stage on which journalism is performed, play a part in how transparency is enacted. All kinds of studies would be welcomed to address the empirical shortage. A few suggestions will be made in the sixth and final chapter of the book.

The public

Transparency is conceptually impossible without the public, because, if you recall the philosophical roots described in Chapter 2, it is about communication between two rational and autonomous actors who have a stake in the outcome of the communication. It literally has no purpose without the public. The contemporary understanding of transparency is closely linked to trust in organizations. If transparency does not have a positive outcome (for the organization) on the public, then it has failed to deliver what was promised and theoretically predicted. It is therefore of utmost importance to map how the public view transparency and the extent to which transparency delivers the anticipated effect.

Considering the importance of the public in the function of transparency, it is ironic that for a long time there were no (although, to be fair, there are now an increasing number of) studies of the role of the public at all. I cannot agree more with what Fenster (2006, p. 928, see also Fenster, 2015) had to say some 15 years ago about the public's request for transparency (in relation to the state): "Transparency theory presumes, in the first instance, the existence of an interested public that needs and wants to be fully informed. This presumption badly needs proof". The same issue was a problem for journalism studies up until a few years ago. It follows that transparency was first raised, then embraced, by industry, professional journalistic organizations, and academics alike (including myself), as a tool with which to repair the declining relationship with the public without sounding out said public systematically. This does not necessarily indicate that the public disapproves of transparency or that there is no positive effect on public trust, but it does imply that the role of transparency in building trust in journalistic institutions remains undefined, and that the transparency norm has been adopted at face value.

As noted in Chapter 1 and above, there are reports of anecdotal evidence that serve to justify the need for transparency. In arguing for the unreleased potential of transparency, McBride and Rosenstiel (2014, p. 89) contend that "We underestimated what information would interest the audience". The yearly NiemanLab predictions earlier witness how audience members across the world are to be considered not only as desiring, but also expecting transparency from the news media, so that they can better understand how news stories are put together. These examples suggest that the public is keen to reduce the information asymmetry in journalism, if only given the chance. That *some* information interests *some* members of the public may very well be true, while at the same time most of the audience is not the least bothered by transparency. Those, from the perspective of the journalistic institution, in most dire "need" of rehabilitation (e.g. non-trustors) might be unmoved or even pushed further away by transparency efforts. More detailed measures are needed to enable the evaluation of the merits and limits of transparency. Luckily, there are an increasing number of empirical studies, primarily surveys and experiments, trying to shine some sunlight on those issues.

Survey research

There is some qualified empirical support for the idea that the public like the idea of transparency. A 2018 Gallup/Knight survey showed that 71 per cent of Americans thought that a news organization's commitment to transparency was important. Transparency tops the list of things that are important for trust in journalism, together with accuracy and lack of bias (Gallup/Knight Foundation, 2018). Similarly, a 2020 report from the Pew Research Centre (Gottfried et al., 2020) explains that 72 per cent of Americans perceive a lack of transparency in news organizations. The report also suggests that the lack of transparency may help to explain the negative evaluation of the news media by Americans. There are thus indications that the public has seen the metaphorical sunshine, and that even more sunshine would restore faith in the journalistic institution.

Other survey studies hint at the limited reach of transparency. Two consecutive papers (van der Wurff & Schönbach, 2014a; van der Wurff & Schönbach, 2014b) noted that although the public expect journalistic transparency, they are also rather conservative in their views of journalistic norms. This suggests that the public does not think that journalism should be that different from its current state. One study (Karlsson et al., 2017) reported that while corrections were appreciated by the Swedish public, they were only effective if the mistakes were small. The effect of transparency (e.g. corrections) is thus contingent on the standard of the original journalistic performance. Moreover, if that standard is high enough (e.g. not in need of correction), then transparency plays a smaller role. The 2020 Pew report (Gottfried et al., 2020) similarly described that a narrow majority of Americans feel more confident in the news when seeing corrections. Equally interesting, a small majority were either unmoved or stated that corrections make them less confident in the news. When asked how well the news media performs transparency, the majority of Americans thought they are doing a poor job, except for corrections.

Experiments

The survey research reported above gives some reason for excitement, as transparency finds relatively strong support among the public. Experimental studies curb that enthusiasm. A 2014 representative Swedish experimental study (Karlsson et al., 2014) tested 20 different transparency scenarios, ranging from hyperlinks to correction, from timestamps to user comments, and more. The most fascinating finding was the almost complete lack of effect. The study did find a few small effects where hyperlinks were used, and that explaining the framing of the article had positive effects, while critical user comments had negative effects. One can wonder whether the lack of effect is a product of Swedish society, which is marked by high interpersonal and institutional trust, thus explaining why there would be little need for the transparency fix. However, a 2017 study in the US (Tandoc & Thomas, 2017) found that transparent news articles were rated as *less* credible than non-transparent articles, suggesting that transparency's lack of appeal extends beyond the particularities of the Nordic welfare states. Another US study (Masullo et al., 2021) investigated whether journalists explaining how and why they covered a news story affected credibility, and found that transparency has a limited effect on credibility, that the results were inconsistent, and that transparency measures really had to stand out to have an effect. Somewhat contrarily, Curry and Stroud (2019) tested five different transparency elements in a US context and found positive outcomes, although the effects in that study were relatively small.

Overall, it is difficult to draw definite conclusions due to the somewhat conflicting results of the experimental studies. It is fairly evident that a more transparent journalism is not having immediate and strong effects, but there are some indications that some part of transparency sometimes appeals to some segments of the public. There are thus reasons to explore the kinds of transparency that different publics want.

... And transparency for all?

Transparency and the public are both commonly viewed as abstract and homogenous entities in the transparency debate (Karlsson, 2020). What kind of transparency would appeal to what kind of public is rarely considered. Plaisance (2007, p. 193) makes a similar observation, stating, "If transparency for the news media means an unthinking process of shovelling everything onto the plates of audiences, journalists would be abdicating their gatekeeper role and most likely undermining the journalistic enterprise in the process". There thus needs to be some kind of selection and prioritizing of transparency, just like any other form of journalistic performance. Adding complexity to the public-centred perspective, Fung et al. (2007) argue that a factor in the success of transparency policies and measures is that they are user-centred (a notion to be further developed in Chapter 6). This means that transparency works better when it is targeted, and "...when they [i.e. information disclosures] provided facts that people wanted in times, places, and ways that enabled them to act" (Fung et al., 2007, p. xiv). A key issue, then, is what the public really wants in the way of transparency. If not everything can be put on the plates of the audience (Plaisance, 2007), the questions remains as to what should be put there. Transparency must be user-centred, but it is unclear what this means more specifically in journalism. If we know little about the public views of transparency in journalism in general, we know almost nothing about transparency with the public's view as a starting point.

In order to identify the kinds of transparency that the public wants, the author, together with a team of researchers, examined the potentially most successful transparency measures in a series of studies (Karlsson et al., 2014; Karlsson & Clerwall, 2018, 2019). Using experiments, surveys, and focus groups, the studies arrived at the conclusion that the most requested transparency features included hyperlinks, using corrections, and explaining news selection and framing.

The overwhelming majority of the previous studies (including those by the author), however, depart from the assumption that transparency is important. They employ transparency techniques that are used by journalistic outlets or proposed by researchers and other actors, and then the public is asked to rate their importance in surveys, or their effects are measured in experiments. This method is closely aligned with the expectations of the implicit theory of transparency – journalists explain what they do, the way they think is best, and ought to be rewarded by trust from the public, which is then measured. That approach, however, assumes that the implicit theory of transparency is accurate. An alternative path into the issue is to let the public decide how important transparency is overall, and which particular aspects of transparency matter, without raising the issues beforehand and having them broken down in detail by researchers.

This line of reasoning was explored in a focus group study, where 82 respondents spread over 13 groups were invited to discuss what constituted "good journalism" for roughly one and a half hours (Karlsson & Clerwall, 2019). The only (initial) task the respondents were charged with was literally to answer the question: "What is good journalism to you?" The respondents were chosen on the basis of their news consumption (high/low) and trust in the news media (high/low), and put in groups with people of similar views: those with low consumption and low trust discussed what "good journalism" is with each other, those with high consumption and low trust discussed with each other, and so forth.

If the implicit theory of transparency is to hold, then transparency as such, or various transparency techniques, should be raised and discussed frequently and with intensity. After all, according to many observers, as detailed previously in the book, the public craves transparency and a more transparent journalism is *the* way to fix the decline in trust of the news media, and thereby make journalism more legitimate (and economically viable). This applies especially to members of the public who consumed little news or had little trust in the news media, since transparency is the medicine that the doctor ordered to sway their opinions. In view of this, the results from the focus groups were staggering. Issues related to transparency were mentioned twice in the sessions, and only in passing. That means that 82 respondents, distributed over 13 focus groups, together spent hour upon hour discussing "good journalism" from their own points of departure, and barely mentioned transparency or the various transparency techniques. Instead of referring to transparency, the respondents thought highly of the much-maligned objectivity ideal (more so in theory than in actual journalistic practice), that journalists should be both audacious and ethical, and that journalism should be easy to read and formulated linguistically correctly (more details can be found in Karlsson & Clerwall, 2019). The various inclinations to transparency that other research has reported might thus be a methodological artefact: that is, in short, the results were provoked by raising the issue.

The different focus groups (high-trust vs low-trust etc.) did not show any differences of opinion. A follow-up study based on an earlier survey tried to tease out the kind of transparency that appealed to different publics (Karlsson, 2020). It found that members of the public who already enjoy journalism likewise appreciate transparency the most. Most transparency measures did not seem to affect those who distrust journalism. In short, people who like journalism like the things that journalism does, others less so. The only exception was some participatory forms of transparency that appealed to the people who were sceptical of journalism. This can be interpreted as people warming to the idea of their own greater involvement, and that of people like them, in journalism, and fewer professional journalists. Another interesting finding was that the participatory forms of journalism that appealed to journalistic sceptics were shunned by those positive towards journalism. It thus seems difficult to please all of the public at once.

Transparency in practice: Not much sunlight thus far

The review of existing research in this chapter shows that transparency falls remarkably short of expectations in at least two ways. First, given the immense interest and high hopes of both academia and the industry in transparency over the last 20 years, the limited number of studies, particularly when it comes to systematic content analysis of major news outlets, is striking. There is also an absence of research examining the delivery and aesthetic dimensions of the transparency performance. The observant reader will note that this chapter has not brought up the "script" dimension of the PTM. This is because there are, to the best of my knowledge, no studies of policies and instructional documents regarding how to enact transparent performance.

Second, the desired effects are dwarfed when compared to the actual outcome. This can depend on several things. Expectations may be too high. Citizens are more attached to the historical trajectory of the journalistic institution than journalists themselves. Transparency may be overrated. Transparency may be enacted in the wrong way. Transparency may be researched in the wrong way. Transparency in journalism may be fundamentally different to transparency in other fields, and we cannot simply import it without considering, and replacing, some of the fundamental assumptions underpinning it.

We will return to this and other issues in the closing chapters, and consider some principal objections to transparency in journalism (Chapter 5) and a few possibly fruitful future research trajectories (Chapter 6). According to the evidence currently available, however, it is quite safe to conclude that transparency, should it work at all, is not quite the quick or easy fix that the implicit theory of transparency would have us believe. More data, sophisticated analysis, and caution are necessary before making claims about how transparency will work for whom.

Notes

1 The metaphor has even given name to the non-profit organization The Sunlight Foundation, which has worked towards transparency in government since 2006. Their mission description is as good as any illustration of the core idea of the implicit theory of transparency: "The Sunlight Foundation is a national, nonpartisan, nonprofit organization that uses civic technologies, open data, policy analysis and journalism to make our government and politics more accountable and transparent to all. Our vision is for technology to enable more complete, equitable and effective democratic participation. Our overarching goal is to achieve changes in the law to require real-time, online transparency for all government information". https://sunlightfoundation.com/ Website visited 14 January 2021.
2 www.newsroomtransparencytracker.com/ Website visited 2 February 2021.
3 A part of the international Pen Network with over a hundred centres around the world advocating issues related to free speech. More information can be found at https://pen.org/about-us/
4 A news consortium funded by Craig Newmark of craigslist, Google, Facebook, and the Knight Foundation, amongst others. More information can be found at https://thetrustproject.org/
5 www.newsguardtech.com/ Website visited 2 February 2021.
6 The fact that a study published 2013, just eight years ago at the time of writing, can justifiably be labelled "early" says something about how new, uncharted, and underdeveloped this research area is.

References

Aronson-Rath, R. (2017). Transparency is the antidote to fake news. www.niemanlab.org/2017/12/transparency-is-the-antidote-to-fake-news/.
Bitterly, K. (2019). *Transparency Isn't Just a Desire, it's an Expectation.* www.niemanlab.org/2019/12/transparency-isnt-just-a-desire-its-an-expectation/.
Brown-Smith, C. (2017). *Transparency Finally Takes Off.* www.niemanlab.org/2017/12/transparency-finally-takes-off/.
Chadha, K., & Koliska, M. (2015). Newsrooms and transparency in the digital age. *Journalism Practice*, 9(2), 215–229. https://doi.org/10.1080/17512786.2014.924737.
Christensen, L. T., & Cornelissen, J. (2015). Organizational transparency as myth and metaphor. *European Journal of Social Theory*, 18(2), 132–149. https://doi.org/10.1177/1368431014555256.
Curry, A. L., & Stroud, N. J. (2019). The effects of journalistic transparency on credibility assessments and engagement intentions. *Journalism*. https://doi.org/10.1177/1464884919850387.

Etzioni, A. (2010). Is transparency the best disinfectant? *Journal of Political Philosophy*, 18(4), 389–404. https://doi.org/10.1111/j.1467-9760.2010.00366.x.

Fenster, M. (2006). The opacity of transparency. *Iowa Law Review*, 91(3), 885–949.

Fenster, M. (2015). Transparency in search of a theory. *European Journal of Social Theory*, 18(2), 150–167. https://doi.org/10.1177/1368431014555257.

Fox, J. (2007). The uncertain relationship between transparency and accountability. *Development in Practice*, 17(4–5), 663–671. https://doi.org/10.1080/09614520701469955.

Fung, A., Graham, M., & Weil, D. (2007). *Full Disclosure: The Perils and Promise of Transparency*. Cambridge University Press. https://doi.org/10.1111/j.1747-1346.2008.00128.x.

Gallup/Knight Foundation. (2018). *Indicators of News Media Trust: A Gallup/Knight Foundation Survey*. https://kf-site-production.s3.amazonaws.com/media_elements/files/000/000/216/original/KnightFoundation_Panel4_Trust_Indicators_FINAL.pdf.

Garcia, M. (2017). *Navigating Journalistic Transparency*. www.niemanlab.org/2017/12/navigating-journalistic-transparency/.

Gottfried, J., Mitchell, A., & Klein, H. (2020). *Americans See Skepticism of News Media as Healthy, Say Public Trust in the Institution Can Improve*. www.journalism.org/2020/08/31/americans-see-skepticism-of-news-media-as-healthy-say-public-trust-in-the-institution-can-improve/.

Grimmelikhuijsen, S. (2012). Linking transparency, knowledge and citizen trust in government: An experiment. *International Review of Administrative Sciences*, 78(1), 50–73. https://doi.org/10.1177/0020852311429667.

Headlee, C. (2020). *The Rise of Radical Newsroom Transparency*. www.niemanlab.org/2020/12/the-rise-of-radical-newsroom-transparency/.

Hedman, U. (2016). When journalists tweet: Disclosure, participatory, and personal transparency. *Social Media and Society*, 2(1). https://doi.org/10.1177/2056305115624528.

Hellmueller, L., Vos, T. P., & Poepsel, M. A. (2013). Shifting journalistic capital? *Journalism Studies*, 14(3), 287–304. https://doi.org/10.1080/1461670X.2012.697686.

Jackson, N. (2018). *More Transparency around Newsroom Decisions*. www.niemanlab.org/2018/12/more-transparency-around-newsroom-decisions/.

Karlsson, M. (2010). Rituals of transparency: Evaluating online news outlets' uses of transparency rituals in the United States, United Kingdom and Sweden. *Journalism Studies*, 11(4), 535–545. www.informaworld.com/smpp/content~db=all~content=a924114735.

Karlsson, M. (2020). Dispersing the opacity of transparency in journalism on the appeal of different forms of transparency to the general public. *Journalism Studies*, 21(3), 1795–1814. https://doi.org/10.1080/1461670X.2020.1790028.

Karlsson, M., & Clerwall, C. (2018). Transparency to the rescue? *Journalism Studies*, 19(13), 1923–1933. https://doi.org/10.1080/1461670X.2018.1492882.

Karlsson, M., & Clerwall, C. (2019). Cornerstones in journalism: According to citizens. *Journalism Studies*, 20(8), 1184–1199. https://doi.org/10.1080/1461670X.2018.1499436.

Karlsson, M., Clerwall, C., & Nord, L. (2014). You ain't seen nothing yet: Transparency's (lack of) effect on source and message credibility. *Journalism Studies*, 15(5), 668–678. https://doi.org/10.1080/1461670X.2014.886837.

Karlsson, M., Clerwall, C., & Nord, L. (2017). Do not stand corrected: Transparency and users' attitudes to inaccurate news and corrections in online journalism. *Journalism & Mass Communication Quarterly*, 94(1), 148–167.

Koliska, M., & Chadha, K. (2018). Transparency in German newsrooms: Diffusion of a new journalistic norm? *Journalism Studies*, 19(16), 2400–2416. https://doi.org/10.1080/1461670X.2017.1349549.

Lasorsa, D. (2012). Transparency and other journalistic norms on Twitter. *Journalism Studies*, 13(2), 402–417. https://doi.org/10.1080/1461670X.2012.657909.

Masullo, G. M., Curry, A. L., Whipple, K. N., Murray, C., Masullo, G. M., Curry, A. L., Whipple, K. N., Murray, C., & Murray, C. (2021). The story behind the story: Examining transparency about the journalistic process and news outlet credibility. *Journalism Practice*. https://doi.org/10.1080/17512786.2020.1870529.

McBride, K., & Rosenstiel, T. (2014). *The New Ethics of Journalism: Principles for the 21st Century*. Sage.

Örnebring, H., Karlsson, M., Fast, K., & Lindell, J. (2018). The space of journalistic work: A theoretical model. *Communication Theory*, 28(4), 403–423. https://doi.org/10.1093/ct/qty006.

Plaisance, P. L. (2007). Transparency: An assessment of the Kantian roots of a key element in media ethics practice. *Journal of Mass Media Ethics*, 22(2–3), 187–207. https://doi.org/10.1080/08900520701315855.

Revers, M. (2014). The Twitterization of news making: Transparency and journalistic professionalism. *Journal of Communication*, 64(5), 806–826. https://doi.org/10.1111/jcom.12111.

Rupar, V. (2006). How did you find that out? Transparency of the news-gathering process and the meaning of news. *Journalism Studies*, 7(1), 127–143. https://doi.org/10.1080/14616700500450426.

Singer, J. (2005). The political j-blogger: "Normalizing" a new media form to fit old norms and practices. *Journalism*, 6(2), 173–198. https://doi.org/10.1177/1464884905051009.

Sullivan, S. (2016). *Baking Transparency Into Our Routines*. www.niemanlab.org/2016/12/baking-transparency-into-our-routines/.

Tandoc, E. C., & Thomas, R. J. (2017). Readers value objectivity over transparency. *Newspaper Research Journal*, 38(1), 32–45. https://doi.org/10.1177/0739532917698446.

van der Wurff, R., & Schönbach, K. (2014a). Civic and citizen demands of news media and journalists: What does the audience expect from good journalism? *Journalism & Mass Communication Quarterly*, 91(3), 433–451. https://doi.org/10.1177/1077699014538974.

van der Wurff, R., & Schönbach, K. (2014b). Audience expectations of media accountability in the Netherlands. *Journalism Studies*, 15(2), 121–137. https://doi.org/10.1080/1461670X.2013.801679.

Vu, H. T., & Saldaña, M. (2021). Chillin' effects of fake news: Changes in practices related to accountability and transparency in American newsrooms under the influence of misinformation and accusations against the news media. *Journalism & Mass Communication Quarterly*. https://doi.org/10.1177/1077699020984781.

Williams, B., & Delli Carpini, M. (2011). *After Broadcast News: Media Regimes, Democracy and the New Information Environment*. Cambridge University Press.

4 Algorithmic forms of transparency and opacity

Chapter 3 analysed and reported on the way transparency has been implemented in traditional modes of journalistic production, distribution, and consumption, and Chapter 4 extends this discussion of transparency to embrace developing areas of research involving artificial intelligence, automation, and algorithms. For simplicity, the word "algorithms" and variations thereof will be used henceforth as a catch-all term for automation, artificial intelligence, and other instances where computer software and hardware affects the production of news. The chapter opens with a brief description of what algorithms are, and an example of an algorithmically produced news story, followed by a description of how algorithms are involved in all important aspects of news production. Algorithms as principal additional black boxes in the newsroom are then discussed. This is followed by an analysis of how the performative transparency model can be used to disentangle and inform the place of algorithms in news production, and how they complicate journalistic performance in terms of transparency. The chapter ends with a discussion linking (semi-) autonomous algorithms to institutional theory and, somewhat speculatively, what it means for transparency when algorithms are self-learning.

Following a trend in society at large, where artificial intelligence and automated decision-making is on the rise, journalism practice and studies have recently moved in the direction of what can be broadly described as the production of journalism in non-journalistic contexts produced by non-journalists. This includes, for instance, how software – popularly called "robot journalism" – has, with some success, taken over parts of a journalist's work, and the robots are programmed by actors outside the usual boundaries of journalism (Anderson, 2011; Carlson, 2015; Clerwall, 2014; Lewis & Westlund, 2015). In this book algorithms are understood, following Kitchin (2017, p. 17), "to be a set of defined steps that if followed in the correct order will computationally process input (instructions and/or data) to produce a desired outcome" (see also Miyazaki, 2012).

DOI: 10.4324/9780429340642-4

I will start by providing an example of algorithmic work that will both serve as an illustration of how such a news item can appear, and later be used as a sounding board to problematize the role of algorithms from a transparency perspective. The following algorithmic work was found in the *Star Tribune*, Minnesota's number one source for local news, by their own account, which published the news item[1] on their website on 5 November 2020:

Correction: Earns-Match Group story
Associated Press
November 5, 2020 – 2:35pm

DALLAS – In a story Wednesday about Match Group Inc.'s quarterly earnings – generated by Automated Insights using data from Zacks Investment Research – The Associated Press reported erroneously that the company's stock declined 48% since the beginning of the year. Match Group began trading as a separate company after a split from IAC Holdings Inc. in July. Shares are up 21% since July 1.

A corrected version of the story is below:
Match Group: 3Q Earnings Snapshot
DALLAS (AP) – Match Group, Inc. (MTCH) on Wednesday reported third-quarter earnings of $132.6 million.

The Dallas-based company said it had profit of 46 cents per share. Earnings, adjusted for one-time gains and costs, were 55 cents per share.

The results fell short of Wall Street expectations. The average estimate of six analysts surveyed by Zacks Investment Research was for earnings of 57 cents per share.

The media and internet company posted revenue of $639.8 million in the period, beating Street forecasts. Seven analysts surveyed by Zacks expected $604.4 million.

Match Group began trading as a separate company after a split from IAC Holdings Inc. in July. Shares are up 21% since July 1.

Elements of this story were generated by Automated Insights (http://automatedinsights.com/ap) using data from Zacks Investment Research. Access a Zacks stock report on MTCH at www.zacks.com/ap/MTCH

This is a typical example of a news story created by algorithms. Since the early 2000s they have become increasingly common, especially in beats like sports, weather, and, as in the example, finance and the economy (Dörr, 2016; Graefe, 2016). Almost all aspects of news gathering, production, distribution, and consumption, as well as all other aspects of life, are in one way or another touched by algorithms (Bucher, 2018; Diakopoulos, 2019).

One intriguing aspect of the news item from the *Star Tribune* is that it is the correction of a previous automatically published news item. It is an algorithmic correction of an algorithmic error, although there is probably more human meddling in the correction than in the original version. It is challenging to distinguish which parts of the news story were created algorithmically and which by humans, based on the information published in the *Star Tribune*. Explaining and showing how news is being made, especially errors and corrections, brings us deep into transparency territory, and algorithms increase the intricacy of those practices.

Algorithms are used to support and supplement the endeavours of human journalists, but they also affect journalistic performances, producing and publishing journalism on their own, not necessarily under direct human supervision. They are thus very much a part of what makes journalism transparent or non-transparent, prompting the question of the extent to which algorithms should be recognized as standalone actors with agency and autonomy of their own (Latour, 2005).

Regardless of whether the introduction and impact of algorithms in journalistic production enforces or breaks with journalistic norms, or has a deep or shallow impact on journalistic practices, it raises significant questions relating to transparency. These questions involve, amongst other things, how much should be revealed and explained about these processes, where they are situated, how the public understands and responds to them, who is actually in charge of them and who is perceived to be in charge of them, and, relatedly, who should be held accountable when, inevitably, technology fails (Carlson, 2018), as illustrated by the example above. This chapter is an effort to tackle those issues.

The increasing role of algorithms in journalism

The key implication of the rise of algorithms in news institutions is not that journalists will be entirely replaced, although there are examples of that too, but the merging of journalists and algorithms into the "human–algorithm system" as Diakopoulos (2019) calls it. The intertwining of humans and algorithms means a broader pattern in restructuring news gathering, production, distribution, and consumption (Bucher, 2018). There is ample research about how various aspects of journalistic work are being conducted with the assistance of algorithms. The topic cannot be extensively covered here, so I will settle for mentioning a few examples so as to argue that algorithms play a role in all important stages of news production, and are, thus, a transparency concern. But first it is crucial to point out that the increased role of algorithms in news production also means that the humans in the human–algorithm system do not necessarily mean *journalists* specifically. It is people in the roles of designers, programmers, and engineers who are likely to make the key decisions about how the system should be programmed, and with what core values (Diakopoulos, 2019). This means that journalists to at least some extent have been displaced from journalism, prompting questions about the training, values, and characteristics of those replacing them.

Algorithms are being used to mine data in databases or on social media in order to find patterns that are interesting from a journalistic perspective, and that would be impossible or very expensive to find if carried out by journalists (Carlson, 2015; Thurman et al., 2016; Wu et al., 2018). Algorithms can for instance be used to identify and notify journalists about topics that are trending or the prevalence of particular words (people, places, etc.) or a source in a corpus. They can also be used to "find the needle in the haystack", which it would be impossible to uncover using basic journalistic techniques (Hansen et al., 2017). Algorithms are thus involved in the *gathering* of news.

In parallel to algorithms mining and scraping data there is also a *selection* process regarding what information it is deemed necessary to forward or not. In journalism studies this selection process is usually given the term "gatekeeping", but in this case, it is the algorithms that, first, "gate-keep" the journalists, and, by proxy, the public. When used for gatekeeping work, algorithms help journalists reduce the noise in, for instance, social media postings, and rank the credibility of the source (Diakopoulos, 2019; Wu et al., 2018). By monitoring a platform and inconsistencies of postings on that platform, algorithms can make journalists aware of newsworthy events, such as the case of the Brussels Airport bombings when Reuters' algorithm gave the news agency an eight-minute head start over its competition due to its ability to identify the event (Thomson Reuters, 2017).

Algorithms are not confined to digging and sorting out information for journalists, however; they can *produce* and publish news stories completely on their own (Carlson, 2015; Dörr, 2016; Napoli, 2014). This takes human journalists out of the loop completely. So far this has been applied in simple and heavily formatted news stories such as economics (as illustrated by the example in the beginning of the chapter), sports, and weather; however, the genres where it is easy to write news stories are also genres where it is easy to scrape data. This means that many news stories are published each day where there is no need, beyond oversight, for human intervention in the news production process (Linden, 2017; Lokot & Diakopoulos, 2016). Furthermore, as will be developed later in the chapter, many of the algorithms producing this news are not situated in-house, making it difficult to explain or even understand how the news items were composed.

Distribution in journalism has often been both costly and unwieldly, as it has required an expensive infrastructure (e.g. broadcasting antenna towers, printing press, lorries, etc.) that has been good at delivering identical content to many people concurrently. Digitalization lowered the threshold, and algorithms allow targeted audiences to be isolated according to interest, topics, geographic location, and previous activities, down to an audience of one (Carlson, 2015; Lokot & Diakopoulos, 2016; Napoli, 2014; Wu et al., 2018). In short, algorithms calculate, predict, and decide to publish news items on different distribution platforms for maximum traction (Bucher, 2018; Diakopoulos, 2019). Algorithms are thus involved in the gathering, selection, processing, and distribution of news. This means that they are entangled in all key steps of journalistic production (Chan-Olmsted, 2019; Domingo et al., 2008; Karlsson, 2011). Given that it was just over a decade ago that algorithms were first implemented in journalism, it is reasonable to expect that future journalism will be even further permeated by them.

If the system that produces news is drastically changed, it will have repercussions for the transparency of that system, notwithstanding that algorithms also allow for other types of journalism that make other social institutions more transparent through rich data sources such as WikiLeaks or the Pulitzer-awarded Panama Paper investigative reporting (see Diakopoulos, 2019, for extensive examples). One aspect is that it will be easier to supplement the data that informs the news, and to make visuals that might be more informative and easier to digest. But the rise of algorithms also leads to changes in the journalistic institution, which may make it less transparent, or at least make transparency more complicated to accomplish.

Russian dolls: Black boxes inside other black boxes, inside...

There is a parallel between the introduction of algorithms in journalism and the decades-old "black box" critique of journalism as a whole (i.e.

that the public cannot see how journalism is made). Algorithms are at the centre of the contemporary debate about black boxing communication and decision-making in general. People are encountering algorithms that shape their everyday experience without being able to access or understand them, but they are aware that algorithms shape their information environments and some people even try to play or reverse engineer the algorithms, and can occasionally see traces of them (Ananny & Crawford, 2018; Diakopoulos, 2019; Kitchin, 2017). Just as algorithms are affecting people's daily lives, there are also algorithmic decisions taken in journalism, both small and big, that are hidden.

On the one hand, as illustrated previously in the book, there are ambitious efforts by industry leaders and professional organizations to transform the newsroom into a transparent "glass box" open to public insight and scrutiny. On the other hand, this will be of less relevance if an increasing amount of journalistic decisions are being determined inside an algorithmic black box. It will, effectively, be a black box located inside a glass box. The net result, regardless of the efforts made to explain journalism to the public, will still be a black box.

Consider the news story in the introduction from a transparency perspective. From the information supplied in the article alone, it emerges that the news item is published by the *Star Tribune* in Minnesota. It is supplied by the Associated Press. It is generated by Automated Insights. It uses data from Zacks Investment Research. At a bare minimum, the information has travelled through four different gates with various institutional logics before it was possible for a *Star Tribune* reader to find it. The net error in the news report is 69 percentage units from the incorrect initial statement that the stock had fallen by 48 per cent to an actual increase of 21 per cent. That is quite a large error.

Now, contemplate the news story from the perspective of fascinated members of the public seeking to understand "how the sausage was made". The implicit theory of transparency assumes there are many such members of the public, or there would be no need for, nor effect from, explaining the news production process. How transparent or opaque are the answers to reasonable questions such as: Where was the error made? Who was responsible? What was the role of the different actors in the process? and What has been done to prevent similar errors from happening again? Is this clear to the public or even to the journalists or editors working on the website? If not, how will they be able to explain it to the public?[2] This is an example of a black box inside a black box inside a black box inside a black box. It is like a Russian doll, however, a Russian doll is easy to unpack since it typically has eight distinct layers, each smaller than the previous one, and it ends with the smallest doll. In algorithms, the dynamics and interdependencies between the different actors/black boxes are obscured and difficult to tease out. They are tesseract Russian dolls. Seaver (2019, p. 419) cautions us about thinking of specific black boxes such as the Google algorithm or the Facebook algorithm as isolated, and instead suggests that "These algorithmic systems are not standalone little boxes, but massive, networked ones with hundreds of hands reaching into them, tweaking and tuning, swapping out parts and experimenting with new arrangements". It is not so much a black box as a black octopus, or a black rhizome. Algorithms are inscrutable in their designs, knowledge thresholds, and principles (Burrell, 2016; Dourish, 2016).

While there has not been an investigation of how the roles of algorithms are explained to the public, and that one example from a news site in Minnesota does not say much for the implementation (and proneness to errors) of algorithms in general, the example raises some fascinating fundamental issues about how algorithmic performances can and should be explained.

Unpacking the role of algorithms in transparent journalistic performance

Chapter 2 detailed some components of journalism – stage, actors, script, aesthetics/delivery, and effects – that are needed in order for transparency to be successfully performed. The rise of algorithms in journalism complicates transparency. It is still definitively a performance on a stage that is open for the public to partake in, but it gets fuzzier when it comes to who the important actors are, what the script is, and who is directing the play.

There are curious similarities between the twenty-first-century algorithmic news performance and earlier mechanical performers. The early eighteenth century saw the rise of automatons. Automatons are mechanical contraptions that simulate aspects of the living original, such as the players of instruments, writers, or, as it were, a defecating duck (Bedini, 1964; Riskin, 2003). In a sense, they are proto-algorithms, as they operated according to a strict manuscript but with enough ability to pass as their living original in some respect. The early automatons consisted of two main parts, a *hidden* machinery made of cogs, pistons, springs, or gears, and a *displayed* animal or human-like figurine, made of materials such as leather, rubber, feather, or cork, which could perform some sort of restricted behaviour. The important thing in terms of transparency is, as Riskin (2003, p. 602) notes, that "the mechanism is all subterranean and the imitative figures all on top". The mechanisms that manage the behaviour of the actors are obscured in a box under the stage, hidden from the view of the public. This was, arguably, very much the basis of the illusion that made automatons amusing and amazing for their contemporary publics. The automatons of the twenty-first century provide a similar illusionary trick. Viewed from PTM, both automatons and algorithms add complexity to the public's need to decode and understand the performance. In the following, I will depart from the components of the PTM to make a few pertinent remarks on the role of algorithms in journalism in relation to transparency.

When it comes to the *stage*, it is evident that the end-product of the algorithmic performance is visible to the public, as news items made by algorithms are published on websites. In that sense the *stage* is probably the least problematic. There are also other times when the work of algorithms is noticeable, such as when, for instance, an advertisement follows you from one news site to another, or the news feed on the mobile phone differs between you and your friend (Bucher, 2018). However, where the actual algorithmic journalism work is performed is less apparent. News stories might be projected onto a news organization's website, just like the example with the *Star Tribune*, but this does not mean they have been gathered, selected, processed, or even assembled there, or that this is the only stage where it is visible, as news is syndicated.

It also raises questions about who is behind the algorithms that produce the news, and to what extent those *actors* are visible on the stage or meaningfully linked to the algorithm and its outcome. Undoubtedly, algorithms are more complicated than eighteenth-century automatons, and more people are involved in their production and performance; however, as with the automatons, the actors directly involved in producing the news, and the performance, are not visible on stage and are thus ghosts to the public. Similarly, Diakopoulous (2019, p. 4, see also Dörr, 2016) observes that not all contributors to the end product are visible but that "…behind the curtain designers, editors, reporters, data scientists, and engineers [are] all contributing in direct or indirect ways". The curtain implicitly refers to Goffman's backstage/frontstage dimensions of a stage. According to Diakopolous, then, there seems to be many things going on backstage, carried out by numerous invisible actors, and making algorithmic journalism less transparent in the process.

The public sees a performance and might ascribe this to journalists or the news organization, but it is not de facto journalists who are behind the performance. Previously I have argued that a key rationale behind transparency is reducing information asymmetry, and that this

work rests heavily on the shoulders of journalists, as they are best positioned to explain news production. With the advent of algorithms, it is
appropriate to ask about the extent to which journalists can even explain
to themselves why event A came out as X instead of Y. If journalists, the
key information asymmetry reducers, cannot do it, then it would be
impossible for the public to do so. It is worth repeating that algorithms
present what can be referred to as "black box challenges", and if they
cannot be overcome, then transparency cannot follow. Following the
increase of actors backstage, it is less clear who is influencing the reporting and how, especially since more than one actor is involved, and they
probably have their hands in more than one black box.

A *script* is intended for journalists to follow and the public to evaluate,
such as codes of ethics or codes of conduct. The increasing role of algorithms means that they are, in one way or another, increasingly affecting
journalism. Questions concerning how the standards of transparent performances are to be communicated and negotiated when journalism is
produced outside the news organizations, and by non-journalists (human
or algorithmic), need to be addressed.

Although algorithms have grown in importance, their role so far is
not recognized by journalistic codes of ethics, which means that there is
no articulated view of, or restrictions on, their place within journalism.
For good measure, we can also compare with sources – understood as
the persons who supply news media with information. Sources are an
important aspect of journalism, in fact, journalism as we know it would
be impossible without them. Despite their paramount importance, sources are looked upon with scepticism. For instance, the SPJ details very
specifically what interactions with sources should look like. Examples
include "Consider the source's motives before promising anonymity"
and "Be wary of sources offering information for favours or money; do
not pay for access to news. Identify content provided by outside sources,
whether paid or not" (Society of Professional Journalists, n.d.). The
interactions between journalists and sources are thus both scripted and
made available for public awareness. This enables the public, at least in
theory, to see what standards journalism is committed to when dealing
with sources, and, consequently, to make up their minds about how
journalism is delivering their self-declared standards. By contrast, there
is currently not a single word about algorithms (or companies providing
algorithms) in the codes of ethics of both the SPJ and RTDNA. Consequently, there is no script, standards, or assessment. In the report by
the Knight Commission on Trust, Media and Democracy (The Aspen
Institute, 2019), algorithms and their role in news are mentioned 35
times, all commenting on how search engines and social media

platforms distort news distribution, creating filter bubbles and echo chambers in the process, and how they should take more responsibility. No attention is given to how the news industry should communicate the role of the algorithms they employ themselves. The transparency issues that inevitably arise from algorithms are thus either not raised or placed outside the boundaries of journalism.

For transparency to achieve the desired effect it must include important elements of *aesthetic and delivery*. There are at least two concerns about algorithms in these respects. The first is how far algorithms themselves are able to intelligibly communicate the rationale behind a publishing decision. The second lies in how news organizations should communicate and explain how, when, why, and what parts of a news story, in terms of gathering, selecting, processing, and distributing the story, are made by non-human entities.

It is certainly possible to shed some light on how algorithms are involved in the news production process, but that does not necessarily mean that this is done on a regular basis (an empirical question waiting to be answered). Another concern is how helpful it is for the public to have the role of algorithms explained to them. Consider the following description (Diakopoulos, 2019, p. 93, see also Diakopoulos & Koliska, 2017) of how the work of algorithms, in this case data-mining, can be transparently explained and made available to the public by means of "…offering descriptions of how the method works, what data it operates from, how constructs are operationalized, what the performance and error rates are on test data, and sometimes even including open source code repositories to facilitate reproducibility". This is technically an apt procedure by which to explain and make the role of algorithms more transparent, but the extent to which a member of the public can, first, decipher the different steps, and then put them together in a meaningful whole is another issue (Burrell, 2016). A further issue is whether they are willing to put in the amount of work needed, should they have the required skills. Similarly, one could ask whether it would have helped the eighteenth-century public understanding of automatons to be shown the clockwork, springs, pistons, and cogs propelling them. Another example, in the journalistic context, is the extent to which trust in journalism in the mid-twentieth century was dependent on a sophisticated understanding of how the printing press, the telegraph, or broadcasting antennas operated. Bucher (2018, p. 41) poignantly makes a general point in this regard: "The question remains as to what exactly it is that should be made transparent and what transparency is believed to help reveal".

My point is that while it may, (and that is a big may), be technically possible to unbox the black box, it is likely that this requires so much from the public that it is still functionally a black box. Maybe it is just easier to trust or distrust that the algorithm, or its proprietor, is doing what it is supposed to do, especially considering the low interest in transparency from the public reported in the previous chapter. To summarize the challenges that algorithms pose for the public in understanding their operations: while the script can be as transparent as possible and the performers able to understand it and therefore able to communicate in a technical sense, aesthetics and delivery are other issues. If the latter are weak, the public is unlikely to pay attention or much interest, meaning that transparency will not have its intended effect.

The *effect* that algorithms have on transparency will be discussed in two ways: first, according to the theoretical effect of algorithms black boxing journalism; and secondly, according to the actual effect that algorithms have on how the public views journalism in terms of trust and trustworthiness.

Starting with the theoretical effect, by now it should be fairly evident that algorithms pose immense challenges to making journalism more transparent, just as algorithms pose great obstacles to transparency in other areas, such as public administration decision-making, dynamic pricing, and prioritization in health care. Currently, there are no standards for explaining the role of algorithms in journalism, and, together with the risk of posting too much information that is too confusing for the public to digest, there is little business incentive to disclose how the algorithms work (Diakopoulos, 2015; Diakopoulos & Koliska, 2017). Add the point made in the section on actors about the increased role of little-known algorithms and their programmers in journalism, and it becomes exceedingly difficult to understand and explain journalism. This makes the ethical challenges of algorithmic journalism almost unsurmountable (see Dörr & Hollnbuchner, 2017, for an excellent overview). It is easy to agree with Just and Latzer (2017, p. 253) and their suggestion that "A high degree of complexity in the cooperation between algorithmic agents and humans results in low transparency (not only for users, as in the mass media, but also for producers), controllability, and predictability compared to reality construction by traditional mass media". Since accurate reality construction is the foundation of journalism's role in society (e.g. informing the public), the implantation of algorithms in news production can have knock-on-effects far beyond the walls of the newsroom. To be blunt, if journalism does not have control or an understanding of why it is producing the output it does, then all those things dependent on journalism, including the informed public required for democracy, are at stake.

Algorithms seem likely to decrease transparency and, according to the implicit theory of transparency, this should then impinge negatively on trust and credibility. This brings us to the actual effects of algorithms, because, strange as it seems, the use of algorithms appears, at least in some cases (Graefe et al., 2018; Sundar & Nass, 2001; Waddell, 2019), to *improve* the credibility of journalism compared to journalism-only authored articles (although see Melin et al. (2018) and Wölker and Powell (2018) for other results). Algorithms are purportedly perceived as more objective than journalists, as the latter are suspected of letting their political preferences determine the news production. This is deceptive, since programming is not neutral, and algorithms are also prone to errors and bias (Diakopoulos, 2019; Graefe et al., 2018). Intriguingly, this improvement in credibility comes despite the opaque ways in which algorithms operate. Less openness in journalistic production results in higher scores in performance. That does not fit well with the implicit theory of transparency; however, it is worth emphasizing that the public perceive the algorithm as more *objective* – rather than less or more *transparent* – and therefore more credible. As seen in the Swedish focus groups and the results from the US experimental study reported in Chapter 3 (Karlsson & Clerwall, 2019; Tandoc & Thomas, 2017), many members of the public value objectivity over transparency. These results indicate that journalism's trust problem might lie in how well it delivers on its objectivity pledge rather than in how it fares on a transparency–opacity scale. We shall return to the transparency–trust relationship in greater detail in Chapter 5.

Computer says no

The basic idea behind transparency in journalism is, to refresh the memory of the reader, to explain how news is made, and how legitimacy is to follow for the social institution in question. Algorithms and the layers of black boxes are a challenge to that. Although there are obvious economic incitements to automate repetitive tasks in news production, those tasks are principally situated *outside* the institution, when done by third, fourth, or fifth parties. These occasionally, but not always, externally owned algorithms are closely guarded business secrets (Bucher, 2018; Burrell, 2016; Diakopoulos, 2019), yet they are very palpably shaping news production processes. It will probably not bode well for transparency, if transparency means explaining how and why news is being made.

If algorithmic journalism is less transparent, this means that those things predicted to follow from transparency – credibility, accountability, legitimacy, and efficacy – are affected too. It might have benefits, such as when the introduction of algorithms increases the credibility of journalism in some cases. When the lead actors (e.g. journalists) are given less or no space to improvise or leave their mark on the performance, the applause (e.g. credibility) from the audience increases. But this also raises the question of the role of the director of the performance, and how to hold them accountable when they are not visible in the performance. If journalists are out of the loop, or at least have less influence in dictating the play, this means that transparency is no longer solely, or even primarily, an issue between the public and journalists, but between the public and *someone* else, whoever and wherever that actor(s) might be. *Someone* else might range from small actors to the big platform/advertising companies of Google, Apple, Facebook, Amazon, and so on. The influence of non-journalistic actors will most likely be greater in smaller news outlets that cannot afford to develop algorithms themselves, and where an algorithm might be the difference between any or no news.

It is true that algorithms so far can only do simple tasks and cannot replace investigative reporting by journalists in the foreseeable future. It is also true that algorithms have more influence on the final appearance of more mundane news such as sports results and stock market reports rather than award-winning journalism of the kind exemplified in the reporting of the Panama papers. However, it does not really matter that algorithms are only riding in the backseat of journalism, since the backseat is still in the car (i.e. the institution). Whatever is produced within journalism, and whenever errors occur – small/large, intentional/unintentional – it impinges on the entirety of the institution. Journalism will not be judged only by hard-hitting political stories, but also by its everyday coverage, of which there is significantly more. Journalism will be judged to the same extent, if not more, by its failures as by its successes and awards. For, as Vos emphasizes (2020, see also Thornton & Ocasio, 2008), institutions *are* their routinized practices (and rules and norms) so what journalism does, and how much control it has over it, is instrumental. Outsourcing and automating news production thus both reshape the institution and let some of the control over it slip away to other actors, who are guided by different routinized practices, rules, and norms.

The black boxing of journalism through algorithms can also be used as a strategic resource (Bucher, 2018); for example, "We cannot know what the algorithm does, do not blame us". My interactions with the *Star Tribune* reported earlier include elements of this. "Yes, we have algorithmic news stories published on *our* website, but *we* don't know how it works. Ask someone else". Well, if transparency is the premier value championed in white papers and codes of ethics, it certainly begs the question of why a tool is employed that removes that value.

Some algorithms can only follow preprogramed paths, while others can learn and improve their performance over time (Bucher, 2018). The learning abilities of self-learning algorithms so far are relatively limited, but issues of transparency will only be more acute in the longer term if the algorithms increase their learning and ability to make autonomous decisions, because one of the outcomes of autonomous machine learning is that it produces behaviour that is unknown to anyone else, meaning that the proprietor of the algorithm is profoundly unable to explain the outcome (Bucher, 2018; Burrell, 2016; Dourish, 2016). The only actant in a position to unpack the algorithmic reasoning and explain why an algorithmically curated news story looks the way it looks is the algorithm itself.[3] When there are several interacting self-learning algorithms involved, the matter will only become more intricate. If asked to elaborate, will the computer say no?

Notes

1 www.startribune.com/correction-earns-match-group-story/572983402/? refresh=true Website visited 20 January 2021.
2 Curious about the answer to that question, I e-mailed the *Star Tribune* (on 22 January 2021), introducing myself as a researcher interested in journalism and transparency, and asking why the error had happened, where it happened and how they work to prevent it from happening again. I helpfully received a swift reply within hours of posing the question. They explained that the AP wires run automatically onto their site and that I would be better off asking them. I did, and I am still (22 March 2021) waiting for a reply.
3 Admittedly, this issue is presently more intriguing in theory than in practice.

References

Ananny, M., & Crawford, K. (2018). Seeing without knowing: Limitations of the transparency ideal and its application to algorithmic accountability. *New Media and Society*, 20(3), 973–989. https://doi.org/10.1177/1461444816676645.

Anderson, C. W. (2011). Deliberative, agonistic, and algorithmic audiences: Journalism's vision of its public in an age of audience transparency. *International Journal of Communication*, 5, 529–547.

Bedini, S. A. (1964). The role of automata in the history of technology. *Technology and Culture*, 5(1), 24–42.

Bucher, T. (2018). *If... Then: Algorithmic Power and Politics*. Oxford University Press.

Burrell, J. (2016). How the machine "thinks": Understanding opacity in machine learning algorithms. *Big Data and Society*, 3(1), 1–12. https://doi.org/10.1177/2053951715622512.

Carlson, M. (2015). The robotic reporter: Automated journalism and the redefinition of labor, compositional forms, and journalistic authority. *Digital Journalism*, 3(3), 416–431. https://doi.org/10.1080/21670811.2014. 976412.

Carlson, M. (2018). Automating judgment? Algorithmic judgment, news knowledge, and journalistic professionalism. *New Media and Society*, 20(5), 1755–1772. https://doi.org/10.1177/1461444817706684.

Chan-Olmsted, S. M. (2019). A review of artificial intelligence adoptions in the media industry. *International Journal on Media Management*, 21(3–4), 193–215. https://doi.org/10.1080/14241277.2019.1695619.

Clerwall, C. (2014). Enter the robot journalist: Users' perceptions of automated content. *Journalism Practice*, 8(5), 519–531. https://doi.org/10.1080/ 17512786.2014.883116.

Diakopoulos, N. (2015). Algorithmic accountability: Journalistic investigation of computational power structures. *Digital Journalism*, 3(3), 398–415. https://doi. org/10.1080/21670811.2014.976411.

Diakopoulos, N. (2019). *Automating the News: How Algorithms Are Rewriting the Media*. Harvard University Press.

Diakopoulos, N., & Koliska, M. (2017). Algorithmic transparency in the news media. *Digital Journalism*, 5(7), 809–828. https://doi.org/10.1080/21670811. 2016.1208053.

Domingo, D., Quandt, T., Heinonen, A., Paulussen, S., Singer, J., & Vujnovic, M. (2008). Participatory journalism practices in the media and beyond. *Journalism Practice*, 2(3), 326–342. https://doi.org/10.1080/17512780802281065.

Dörr, K. N. (2016). Mapping the field of algorithmic journalism. *Digital Journalism*, 4(6), 700–722. https://doi.org/10.1080/21670811.2015.1096748.

Dörr, K. N., & Hollnbuchner, K. (2017). Ethical challenges of algorithmic journalism. *Digital Journalism*, 5(4), 404–419. https://doi.org/10.1080/21670811.2016. 1167612.

Dourish, P. (2016). Algorithms and their others: Algorithmic culture in context. *Big Data & Society*, 3(2). https://doi.org/10.1177/2053951716665128.

Graefe, A. (2016). *Guide to Automated Journalism*. https://doi.org/10.7916/ D80G3XDJ.

Graefe, A., Haim, M., Haarmann, B., & Brosius, H. B. (2018). Readers' perception of computer-generated news: Credibility, expertise, and readability. *Journalism*, 19(5), 595–610. https://doi.org/10.1177/1464884916641269.

Hansen, M., Roca-Sales, M., Keegan, J., & King, G. (2017). *Artificial Intelligence: Practice and Implications for Journalism*. Tow Center for Digital Journalism.

Just, N., & Latzer, M. (2017). Governance by algorithms: Reality construction by algorithmic selection on the internet. *Media, Culture & Society*, 39(2), 238–258. https://doi.org/10.1177/0163443716643157.

Karlsson, M. (2011). The immediacy of online news, the visibility of journalistic processes and a restructuring of journalistic authority. *Journalism*, 12 (3), 279–295. https://doi.org/10.1177/1464884910388223.

Karlsson, M., & Clerwall, C. (2019). Cornerstones in journalism: According to citizens. *Journalism Studies*, 20(8), 1184–1199. https://doi.org/10.1080/1461670X.2018.1499436.

Kitchin, R. (2017). Thinking critically about and researching algorithms. *Information Communication and Society*, 20(1), 14–29. https://doi.org/10.1080/1369118X.2016.1154087.

Latour, B. (2005). *Reassembling the Social: An Introduction to Actor-Network-Theory*. Oxford University Press.

Lewis, S. C., & Westlund, O. (2015). Actors, actants, audiences, and activities in cross-media news work. *Digital Journalism*, 3(1), 19–37. https://doi.org/10.1080/21670811.2014.927986.

Linden, C. G. (2017). Decades of automation in the newsroom: Why are there still so many jobs in journalism? *Digital Journalism*, 5(2), 123–140. https://doi.org/10.1080/21670811.2016.1160791.

Lokot, T., & Diakopoulos, N. (2016). News bots: Automating news and information dissemination on Twitter. *Digital Journalism*, 4(6), 682–699. https://doi.org/10.1080/21670811.2015.1081822.

Melin, M., Bäck, A., Södergård, C., Munezero, M., Leppänen, L., & Toivonen, H. (2018). No landslide for the human journalist: An empirical study of computer-generated election news in Finland. *IEEE Access*, 6, 43356–43367.

Miyazaki, S. (2012). Algorhythmics: Understanding micro-temporality in computational cultures. *Computational Culture*, 2, 1–16.

Napoli, P. M. (2014). Automated media: An institutional theory perspective on algorithmic media production and consumption. *Communication Theory*, 24(3), 340–360. https://doi.org/10.1111/comt.12039.

Riskin, J. (2003). The defecating duck, or, the ambiguous origins of artificial life. *Critical Inquiry*, 29(4), 599–633. https://doi.org/10.1086/377722.

Seaver, N. (2019). Knowing algorithms. *Digital STS*, 412–422. https://digitalsts.net/wp-content/uploads/2019/03/26_Knowing-Algorithms.pdf.

Society of Professional Journalists. (n.d.). *SPJ Code of Ethics*. www.spj.org/ethicscode.asp.

Sundar, S. S., & Nass, C. (2001). Conceptualizing sources in online news. *Journal of Communication*, 51(1), 52–72. https://doi.org/10.1111/j.1460-2466.2001.tb02872.x.

Tandoc, E. C., & Thomas, R. J. (2017). Readers value objectivity over transparency. *Newspaper Research Journal*, 38(1), 32–45. https://doi.org/10.1177/0739532917698446.

The Aspen Institute. (2019). *The Report of the Knight Commission on Trust, Media and Democracy: Crisis in Democracy: Renewing Trust in America*. http://as.pn/trust.

Thomson Reuters. (2017). *The Making of Reuters News Tracer*. https://blogs.thomsonreuters.com/answerson/making-reuters-news-tracer/.

Thornton, P. H., & Ocasio, W. (2008). Institutional logics. In R. Greenwood, C. Oliver, R. Suddaby & K. Sahlin (Eds.), *The SAGE Handbook of Organizational Institutionalism* (pp. 99–128). Sage. https://doi.org/10.4135/9781849200387.n4.

Thurman, N., Schifferes, S., Fletcher, R., Newman, N., Hunt, S., & Schapals, A. K. (2016). Giving computers a nose for news: Exploring the limits of story detection and verification. *Digital Journalism*, 4(7), 838–848. https:// doi.org/10.1080/21670811.2016.1149436.

Vos, T. (2020). Journalism as institution. In H. Örnebring (Ed.), *The Oxford Encyclopedia of Journalism Studies* (pp. 736–750). Oxford University Press.

Waddell, T. F. (2019). Can an algorithm reduce the perceived bias of news? Testing the effect of machine attribution on news readers' evaluations of bias, anthropomorphism, and credibility. *Journalism & Mass Communication Quarterly*. https://doi.org/10.1177/1077699018815891.

Wölker, A., & Powell, T. E. (2018). Algorithms in the newsroom? News readers' perceived credibility and selection of automated journalism. *Journalism*. https:// doi.org/10.1177/1464884918757072.

Wu, S., Tandoc, E. C., & Salmon, C. T. (2018). Journalism reconfigured: Assessing human–machine relations and the autonomous power of automation in news production. *Journalism Studies*. https://doi.org/10.1080/ 1461670X.2018.1521299.

5   The limits of the transparency myth

Who could genuinely say that they oppose transparency?[1] It certainly sounds good in theory – providing citizens with more information so that they can evaluate the performance of journalism (and other social institutions) for themselves. Everyone seems to cheerfully agree and with little, if any, hesitation. Journalists' professional organizations have changed their norms. Industry leaders sign up to the concept. Academics chime in. It is a norm widely hailed by society at large. There are signs that the public agree to it in principle. However, while transparency is supposed to gain the public's trust in journalism by showing how it is made, there are meagre returns on this, as detailed in Chapter 3. This raises the question of the extent to which the public's distancing from journalism is a sausage-making-knowledge problem to begin with. In short, despite widespread consensus that transparency *should* work as a trust-generating measure, there is little empirical evidence that it *does* work in this way. In that sense, transparency has achieved mythical status as a taken-for-granted and celebrated ideal that has moved beyond the realm of critical scrutiny (Christensen & Cornelissen, 2015; Meyer & Rowan, 1977). This, in turn, questions the relevance of the theoretical assumptions underlying transparency. Chapter 5 engages with some of those theoretical assumptions.

This chapter is divided into five sections. The first section considers the inevitable trade-offs that are involved once limited resources are channelled from one area of a business to another, such as starting to do things more transparently and, consequently, stopping doing other things that might be unrelated to, or equally or more important to, the legitimacy of the institution. This is followed by a discussion of the seemingly inherent conflict between professional discretionary decision-making and transparency. In short, there is a conflict between control and openness. I make the point that wherever there is a performance there will be a curtain and a backstage, thus evoking questions of what

DOI: 10.4324/9780429340642-5

is still concealed and why, despite claims of transparency. I introduce a broader theoretical discussion about the innate conflict between the concepts of trust and transparency. In brief, the kernel of this conflict is based on the idea that a person trusts another person or institution in the absence of evidence and that transparency is essentially about presenting evidence in a fashionable way. After this argument, I revisit the discussion of "transparency = openness", as hitherto understood by journalism scholars, and argue that this is misleading, and that it is more useful to recognize transparency as a strategically managed visibility. I also argue why it is crucial to consider this distinction in view of transparency's inability to generate trust. The final section of the chapter uses institutional theory to propose an explanation of why transparency so far has been embraced by prominent actors in the institution, despite being a failure in terms of addressing the problems it is supposedly designed to solve.

Inevitable cost/benefit trade-offs

Journalism practice and studies rarely consider the cost/benefit ratio or the net gain of transparency. When transparency is discussed there is an emphasis on what can be achieved (e.g. increased credibility, stronger relationships with readers), but rarely is the unavoidable resource allocation acknowledged or discussed. This is necessary, as the performance of transparency involves "transactional and informational costs" (Ball, 2009, p. 300, see also Etzioni, 2010) and needs backing. Regardless of whether transparency is applied in a public or commercial organization, the resources required to deliver it need to come from "somewhere". Unless that somewhere is a completely unnecessary part of the institution, it may crucially have an equally or more important function in achieving public trust. We would, for instance, be more inclined to trust a garage that fixed our vehicle, even if we did not know exactly how, rather than being given a lecture about why a repair was not possible, or how it would only have been possible in a different way.

Compared to alternative institutional activities, measures of transparency may therefore neither receive the same recognition, nor produce an equal or better effect. For instance, in an experimental study, Curry and Stroud (2019) offered interactive transparency elements for respondents to engage with. According to the implicit theory of transparency, this provided ample opportunity for the respondents to look behind the curtain; however, the study noted that very few even bothered to click on the elements. The next step from a cost/benefit perspective would be to calculate the cost of producing and maintaining those transparency elements with the estimated net benefit of the interaction for a limited segment of the public. Given that disclosure transparency appeals to those who already trust journalism (Karlsson, 2020), it would be useful to identify the segment of the public that interacted with the transparency features, and the reputational and economic benefit.

Let us expand this reasoning and take a hypothetical scenario involving errors and corrections to make a case in point. Obviously, it is impossible to put an exact price tag on different parts of the journalistic work process, so this example is a metaphor for the principal problem and offered as a thought exercise.

Journalists and citizens alike think that avoiding errors when reporting the news should be the first priority and correcting them should be the second priority. When journalists do make errors, trust is thus lost that corrections cannot fully compensate (Karlsson et al., 2017). In our hypothetical scenario, a news organization decides to launch an ambitious transparency program that includes a pedagogical system for addressing corrections. To get this transparency program up and running, people across the organization need to work many extra hours. New software needs to be bought and implemented within the existing content management system. Consultants are hired. There are calibrations with other news organizations going through similar procedures (using the same consultants and software). In short, the news organization decides to use some of its limited resources to build a bureaucratic infrastructure dedicated to transparency. To accomplish all this, resources are pulled from other parts of the organization, including the newsroom (after all, the expected net effect will be positive). This leads to fewer hours channelled into original reporting and fact-checking, which, in turn, presumably leads to more errors that must be corrected. The increased number of errors presumably has a negative impact on how far citizens trust the news outlet. The transparency measurement that was designed to increase trust thus had the opposite actual effect (e.g. Curtin & Meijer, 2006).

In an ideal scenario, the implementation of transparency is so successful that the organization acquires more monetary and/or symbolic resources than it would otherwise have, which can be invested in good journalism appealing to the public and advertisers alike and increasing the legitimacy and turnover of the institution. In other words, the effort put into providing transparency will create a net gain. However, for this to happen both the costs and benefits of transparency need to be measured, no matter how complicated that would be in practice.[2] There are many possible transparency measurements, and they probably have different costs and benefits both on their own, and together with other measurements. For instance, the implementation of corrections and explaining the news selection process might have value individually, but their added value might be more or less than the sum of the parts.

The literature does not often report such reflections or calculations, as it is usually the *potential* benefits that are considered, rather than the *inevitable* transactional and informational costs (Ball, 2009). It is also a question of how a tentative transparency net gain for one organization can be applied to other organizations or across the entire social institution. In the context of journalism, one could reasonably ask whether local newspapers, elite national media, news aggregators, public service broadcasters, and gossip sites, to mention a few examples, have the same cost/benefit ratio.

Finally, we need to identify the actors that really benefit from transparency. In theory, transparency is there to serve the public, but policy research (Fung et al., 2007) demonstrates that right-to-know policies were by far most commonly used by businesses trying to obtain information about other businesses. Individuals or public interest groups only comprised 1 per cent of the requests. A 2006 study (Curtin & Meijer, 2006) demonstrated that the ratio of EU citizens who had exercised their right of information compared to those who had not was 1:33,000. Yes, for every citizen who searched for information in the EU, there were 33,000 who did not. These numbers are not necessarily translatable into journalism, but it raises the important issues of who the transparency is for, who is interested, who it is that will eventually benefit from it, what the costs are, and what the resources could have been used for otherwise.

The need for professional discretion and the ever-present curtain and backstage

The debate on transparency places considerable weight on the idea that it can – no, should – lead to greater credibility and legitimacy, increasing manoeuvrability for both the individual worker and the organization. However, theoretically, as with any other ethical rule or code of conduct, transparency can also undermine the manoeuvrability of professionals, because, as argued by organizational scholars Levay and Waks (2009, p. 510), "Professionals have an interest in keeping their work opaque to outsiders in order to safeguard their freedom of discretion, both as individual practitioners and as organized occupational groups". This was noted by some of Revers' (2014) journalist respondents, who found that transparency means giving up some of the professional discretion that is at the heart of professional autonomy. These issues have been discussed in journalism studies under the headings of boundary work and boundary maintenance (Carlson, 2016; Lewis, 2012). A central problem of boundary work is the issue of demarcation (Gieryn, 1983), that is, who decides what passes as belonging inside the journalistic institution (in Gieryns case, science) and what must stay on the outside, as non-journalism. This boundary maintenance is not only a question for individual journalists, or their profession, but for the institution as a whole.

Chapter 1 referred to institutional theory and noted that "An institution is constituted by routinized practices, implicit and explicit rules, and explicit norms" (Vos, 2020, p. 726). Boundary work is also carried out in the daily actions of the institution, and Gieryn (1983, p. 781) explains that "demarcation is routinely accomplished in practical, everyday settings" such as when schools include evolutionary theory but not creationism in the curricula, when health care authorities certify penicillin but not homeopathy as a legitimate medicine to treat infections, or the way journalism separates news from opinion, which in turn is separated from advertising. A social institution that has a high level of autonomy will not only be able to choose how to carry out its work daily, hence *maintaining* the lines of demarcation, but also set up the overarching and long-term rules that ultimately *govern* the lines of demarcation (Örnebring & Karlsson, forthcoming). Thus, when the discretion to choose how to do the work and set up the rules for doing so is undermined, the social institution as such is also potentially undermined. There might be good reasons for doing so, if a local and short-term dent in autonomy leads to a general and long-term strengthening of autonomy, legitimacy, and authority. This is the line of argument in the implicit theory of transparency put forward by the proponents of transparency: by changing norms and practices that have historically served journalism so well in favour of norms and practices that are transparent, increased trust and with that legitimacy will follow. Here also lies a risk. When giving up discretion and letting others dictate/influence how things are done, journalists and news organizations could be seen as puppets, with little legitimacy and authority of their own, facing the question "You used to be about this, now it is this, what do you really stand for?" Being inconsistent and making changes that are too big, too quick, or too frequent, places organizations at risk of being viewed as hypocritical or unreliable (Fredriksson & Edwards, 2019).

In tandem with the discussion on professional discretionary decision-making is the issue of moving the lines regarding what should be transparent. Transparency, by definition, tilts the discussion towards openness and frontstage behaviour, as the focus lies on what is now exposed but was previously hidden, but there will always be a need for backstage behaviour, as bureaucracies need institutional secrecy to operate (Curtin & Meijer, 2006; Fenster, 2006; Fredriksson & Edwards, 2019; Rourke, 1957), and wherever that line is drawn, there will always be two sides to it, setting up yet another curtain demarcating what is frontstage and backstage (Flyverbom, 2016; Karlsson, 2011). There will always be non-transparent things, as not everything can be on display.

Transparency measures themselves also have a non-transparent quality. In the case of corrections, it is literally impossible for the public to *know* (beyond minor errors like spelling or misnaming persons or places) that this or that piece of information was incorrect at the first instance but has now been corrected by well-intentioned journalists. All they have with which to evaluate both the original error and the following correction (and any other activity from journalists), is at best hand-me-down knowledge. Although the stage can be ever expanded, therefore, there is still an area backstage which the spotlights do not reach.

Relatedly, any successful profession offers something that the public entrust them to do (a point to which we shall soon return). While the public can certainly offer criticism or alternative views, the core of a profession[3] cannot be explained or comprehended by the public (or professional knowledge would not be exclusive) and the public accepts that (or they would not trust the profession). Reformulating the issue in terms of the PTM it is acceptable that some things remain backstage behind the curtain. Reversing the transparency argument, then, it is necessary to ask – what kind of institutional secrecy is a functional necessity for professional journalism?

Transparency as the opposite of trust

A great deal of theorizing on the connection between transparency and trust departs from an *a priori* position that there is both a positive link between transparency and trust, and a clear direction of causality. When transparency increases, so does trust. When transparency decreases, so does trust. In fact, this is the quintessential idea underpinning the need for discussion in the first place. Despite the nearly unanimous view about the positive causal relationship, there are reasons for caution. As we have seen, there is little empirical evidence that increased transparency leads to increased trust. This could, on the one hand, be due to inefficient transparency measures implemented by journalism, or research being conducted the wrong way or any other "technical" reason. In this view, the basic idea of transparency still holds, but we have not yet cracked the code concerning how it should be performed. Tuning the script, swapping stages, touching up the aesthetics, or replacing an actor or two is thought to do the trick. However, on the other hand, there are some objections on the grounds of principles to the nature of the transparency–trust bond. In the following, I will visit some ideas from thinkers who have a different take on the relationship, but first we need to consider what trust is.

There are two preconditions for trust: uncertainty and vulnerability (Hall et al., 2001; Lewis & Weigert, 1985; Mayer et al., 1995). If people knew everything they wanted or needed to know, then it would not be necessary to turn to others. The moment we turn to others for help orienting ourselves in the world, uncertainty and vulnerability follow, uncertainty because we do not have first-hand knowledge, and vulnerability because we open ourselves to others to take advantage of our exposed position. Trust, then, fills the dual purpose of replacing knowledge and reducing uncertainty (Kohring & Matthes, 2007). What is intriguing in the context of transparency is that trust is not founded on knowledge, but on the absence of it. Lewis and Weigert (1985, p. 970) explain that "The manifestation of trust on the cognitive level of experience is reached when social actors no *longer need or want any further evidence or rational reasons* for their confidence in the objects of trust" (author's italics). Regardless of the evidence or explanations, there is thus a point when a person *must* make a leap of faith in the absence of evidence, because as philosopher Onora O'Neill explains (O'Neill, 2002, p. 6), at some point we have to trust because "[g]uarantees are useless unless they lead to a trusted source, and a regress of guarantees is no better for being longer unless it ends in a trusted source". Thus, there is no way of evading the leap of faith, and additional guarantees, evidence and explanations cannot replace the leap of faith but merely push it further ahead. Since transparency is about explaining and providing facts about the true nature of the inner workings of institutions, it raises the question of the extent to which it provides a platform from which to make that leap of faith, or whether it takes the platform out of the equation entirely (Schoorman et al., 2007). Another issue is the extent to which the distrust in news media rests on rational foundations that transparency seeks to address, or emotional attachments and moods (Grimmelikhuijsen, 2012; Lewis & Weigert, 1985; Schoorman et al., 2007).

On a similar note, social thinker Richard Sennett (2003, p. 122f) observes the inequality between rulers and ruled, and the contradiction between trust and transparency. For the purpose of this book, I suggest that this is comparable to other relationships where there is information asymmetry between someone in a position of power (e.g. news media) and someone who is not (e.g. the public) (Alt et al., 2002; Ball, 2009; Fung et al., 2007). Sennett's argument is worth quoting at length:

> The people have to believe in and trust their ruler; when they trust, they grant him a measure of freedom to act without constant auditing, monitoring, and oversight [e.g. without transparency]. Lacking that autonomy, he could indeed never make a move. The intellectual drama of liberalism lies partly in the way this acceptance of autonomy conflicts with belief in rational judgement. Sympathy fits into rational, transparent acts of consent; the citizen and ruler should be able to identify with the experience of the other [e.g. disclosure and reciprocity]. Lack of mutual understanding invites abuse of power. Yet without the citizen's granting of autonomy to the ruler, the state, like the family, will break down.

Here, Sennett points out the conflict between efficacy and transparency. Unless the ruler (in our case the person at the upper side of information asymmetry) is given freedom to act without transparency nothing will happen, yet without transparency there is the evident risk of abuse of power. Sennett (2003, p. 122) goes on to argue about the distinction between "a transparent equality" and "an opaque equality". The former is based on an equality of knowledge – that is, levelling information asymmetry. The latter means to accept what one does not understand, as in the case with doctors or teachers where we can understand that *they* know what they are doing, but that *we* do not *know* what they are doing. We thus grant them autonomy to do what they do through this acceptance, or leap of trust. Consequently, for journalists to be autonomous (and the public too for that matter) they need some opacity, or professional discretion, of their own.

In view of this, the finding reported in Chapter 4 that people trust algorithms more than human journalists, is intriguing. Assuming that the respondents in those studies did not have degrees in computer science, they are willing to accept that things they do not understand (e.g. algorithms) are worthy of trust; opaque equality, using Sennett's term. Departing from Sennett's argument that granting others autonomy means accepting what you do not understand, then it follows that algorithms are in some cases granted more autonomy than human journalists.

If we take our guidance from Sennett, the conflict between autonomous journalism and transparency means that the information asymmetry which transparency is supposed to address cannot be fully solved if the institution is to remain autonomous. Since the point of transparency is to secure an institution's social authority and legitimacy (by acquiring trust) so that it can continue to be autonomous and prosper, the question remains as to whether this is even theoretically possible. Going even further, philosopher Byung-Chul Han (2015, p. 48) raises an existential question about transparency, and proposes that transparency cannot lead to trust because transparency is the opposite of trust. Embracing transparency means:

> Where transparency prevails, no room for trust exists. Instead of affirming that "transparency creates trust", one should instead say, "transparency dismantles trust". The demand for transparency grows loud precisely when trust no longer prevails. In a society based on trust, no intrusive demand for transparency would surface. The society of transparency is a society of mistrust and suspicion: it relies on control because of vanishing confidence.

Trust is the acceptance of being vulnerable when facing uncertainty. Transparency aims to reduce uncertainty. If, then, trust is a leap of faith, something that one does *despite* a lack of, or deficiencies in, openness, evidence or assurance, then transparency rescinds trust as it aims to reduce the opportunity to make that leap of faith. Transparency is in this sense in contrast to trust. The endgame of transparency is, from this viewpoint, to make trust redundant. In any case, it certainly cannot be used to increase trust since that would be asking people to make bigger leaps of faith while working frantically to reduce the gap that they must jump. On the one hand, therefore, transparency is literally worthless. On the other hand it will supposedly save society and the institutions within it. Yet again, there is the evidence that we saw in Chapter 3, suggesting that transparency has a small but real positive effect on trust for some people. So where in the world does that leave us? It leaves us with an opportunity to move forward with more meticulous research agendas, some of which are presented in Chapter 6.

Transparency is not openness

Usually, when trying to condense the concept of transparency to its core value, researchers translate it as openness (Etzioni, 2010; Heim & Craft, 2020; Karlsson, 2010; Plaisance, 2007; Vos & Craft, 2017). While transparency has elements of openness, there are other forms of openness, most prominently freedom of information, that are something different compared to transparency.

In Chapters 1 and 2 we found that transparency has a specific purpose, for a specific actor in a specific context. Transparency is intended to increase (or maintain) an institution's authority and legitimacy in circumstances under which they have an information advantage over the public. To do so, transparency is performed with varying amounts of effectiveness, measured according to the goal of the organization. Performances are scripted for maximum effectiveness, and so they are consequently delivered under the precondition that they can be controlled, and that control is desirable. This control presumes that the organization has comprehensive self-knowledge, otherwise it would not know what to be transparent about (Fredriksson & Edwards, 2019).

Since transparency has an element of control, it is also a sibling to secrecy, because as Fenster (2015, p. 156) noted, "Secrecy and transparency both require the power to control information...", and, I argue, this is not only about power but also about the *ability* to channel and deliver the information in a comprehensible manner. This is at the gist of the performative transparency model. Relatedly, transparency *must* be managed, because providing a plethora of information is not immensely helpful if the purpose of transparency was for the organization to *explain* its behaviour (e.g. establishing some sort of narrative or performance). As Plaisance (2007) notes, transparency is a gatekeeping activity. We can compare this to freedom of information legislation which gives people the right to access information on their own. Of course, the information that they can access is managed too, but it is not staged, scripted, cast, and read out loud by an actor from the institution, which is what transparency *performance* means. Both freedom of information laws and transparency are about disclosure, but there are fundamental differences in the core objectives of the openness. The purpose behind freedom of information is to make information available to the public for their own use. The purpose behind the contemporary avowal of transparency is to increase the social legitimacy and authority of the institution.

Against this background, transparency is in my view better and more honestly understood as *strategically managed visibility* (see also Flyverbom, 2016). The word "strategic" indicates that transparency ultimately has a purpose for an institutional actor, whether it involves the shorter-term goal of "increasing trust" or the longer-term goal of using "authority and legitimacy" to sustain its further operations. If research showed that transparency decreased trust considerably, surely the idea would be dropped as quickly as yesterday's news. Visibility reveals the unavoidable co-existence of the hidden and displayed, the backstage and the frontstage, and that where things end up is not governed by randomness. Being managed uncovers, for good and bad, the controlled and scripted nature of the performance, and the ambition to tune it for the purpose of organization. It can be argued that increased openness (i.e. transparency) mobilizes managers to increase control over information flows, because a too-unrestrained organization risks taking inconsistent and contradictory decisions that negatively affect the perception of the organization (Fredriksson & Edwards, 2019).

If this line of reasoning sounds familiar, that is perhaps because you have read it before. This is basically a slightly reformulated argument based on Tuchman's notion of objectivity as a strategic ritual (Tuchman, 1972). The ritual is performed defensively to keep the most salient public at bay. That public is not necessarily "the public" but other actors inside and outside the institution with leverage on the institution's future direction. This is also remarkably similar to the case of transparency and its strategic use. It is rhetorically taken aboard to strengthen the relationship with the public, but the public have never been systematically sounded out. The reason that transparency is adopted despite the lack of evidence supporting the role it is rhetorically supposed to have will be addressed under the next subheading.

In parallel with this, and to revisit a discussion from earlier in the chapter, transparency and professional control are not necessarily in conflict with each other. Information asymmetry and the performative nature of transparency let at least someone in the institution have more command over the situation than those on the outside. It might very well be different forms and expressions of control demanding new skills and practices, but it is still about control at heart. Moreover, that control might not lie in the hands of the journalistic profession.

Transparency understood as strategically managed visibility raises the issue of the guiding logic behind transparency and its origin, the role that *intention* plays in that process, and how that plays into trust. Remember that Plaisance (2007, p. 188, see also Vos & Craft, 2017) anchored transparency in Kantian ethics and defined it as a "conduct that presumes an openness in communication and serves a reasonable *expectation* of *forthright* exchange when parties have a legitimate stake in the possible outcomes or effects of the communicative act" (author's italics). For transparency to take place, trust must therefore already be in place, as there are expectations of well-meant or non-hostile intentions. From this it also follows that when there are no expectations of forthrightness (e.g. mistrust), transparency is in trouble.

A transparent performance is a scripted performance, and the script is written by someone. If the disclosure of an allegedly behind-the-scenes peek is operated by a person or institution that you do not trust (e.g. is expected to be insincere rather than forthright), then little is changed in the principle of who controls the information flow, and with what perceived intentions. One could reasonably question why a sceptic's trust would change and why they would willingly take a leap of faith just because an institution they mistrust releases more information. The functionalistic linearity of the implicit theory of transparency is thus revealed: if only there were perfectly worded messages transmitted in sufficient numbers, then the unfounded mistrust would dissipate. If this was translated into an empirical question, it might ask: How many pedagogical messages explaining how journalism works must a person who distrusts news media receive before being swayed? When explicitly stated in this way, it might seem somewhat odd, but this is one of the underlying assumptions guiding the implicit theory of transparency. It puts us back in the territory of the conflicting natures of trust and transparency. At some point the sceptics and non-trustors must take a leap of faith despite the lack of insight and guarantees. Alternatively, and perhaps more plausibly, they will not make the leap of faith at all, and continue to distrust.

It is worth highlighting/repeating the findings of a study comparing the kinds of transparency that appealed to different kinds of people (Karlsson, 2020). The kind of transparency that appealed to people who mistrusted journalists was participatory transparency; that is, forms of transparency where journalists are less involved, and, presumably, people like themselves were more involved. Similarly, those with the most positive outlook on features of transparency already trusted journalism. It thus seems that trust and transparency are interlocked in a reinforcing spiral. Then again, if one already trusts journalism, transparency is superfluous.

A successful flop: How transparency was adopted despite a lack of evidence

Transparency is an enigmatic topic. On the one hand, it has made its way into the core of journalism in just a decade. One the other hand, it does not seem to work very well. Squeezing those two equally true but disparate observations into one statement, transparency can be described as a successful flop. But if transparency does not deliver the goods, the question remains as to why, then, various members of journalistic and neighbouring institutions are singing its praises. In this regard, institutionalist theoreticians DiMaggio and Powell (1983, p. 147, see also Meyer & Rowan, 1977) make a very interesting point when explaining the directions in which organizations evolve, and especially concerning organizational isomorphism. They argue that "...bureaucratization and other forms of organizational change occur as the result of processes that make organizations more similar without necessarily making them more efficient". Here is a possible explanation of why institutions such as journalism embrace transparency when it does not make them more efficient (i.e. increasing trust or circulation).

DiMaggio and Powell (1983, p. 154ff) hypothesize that several conditions predict increased isomorphism, and presumably increase bureaucratization. A few of these fit very well with the trajectory of journalism. Generally, organizations will model themselves after other organizations they deem successful. This isomorphism will accelerate with, to highlight a few of the reasons and illustrate how it can be interpreted in relation to journalism: the ambiguity of organizational goals (journalism: inform the public); increased reliance on academic credentials (journalism: graduate schools); level of managerial engagement in trade and professional organizations (journalism: SPJ, RTDNA, ASNE); high levels of interaction with state agencies (journalism: institutionalized sourcing to the extent that the news media have their own press galleries in parliament); and technology-induced uncertainty (journalism: disrupted distribution flows and advertising revenue due to search engines and social media networks).

Once an idea has entered the field and taken root, processes of homogenization follow, because "[t]his process encourages homogenisation as organisations seek to ensure that they can provide the same benefits and services as their competitors" (DiMaggio & Powell, 1983, p. 154). Thus, by following the normative shift in society towards transparency and mimicking institutions of high standing and normative pressure from professional bodies (inside and outside the journalistic field), journalism is more likely to walk down the path of transparency and become more bureaucratized in the process. Once the "fix is in" there is a market for consulting, keynotes, education, and the measurement of different expressions of transparency. The rankings and various initiatives, commercial and non-commercial, thus offer rudimentary transparency audits, providing a score or badge announcing whether an outlet is transparent or not, for a few measly dollars every month. *Newsguard* rates the transparency and credibility of sites as green (good), red (bad), satire (not news), and platform (another category of "not news"). The startup *Credder* is, in their own words, "the world's largest news review platform" and offers news organizations a "partner program" with somewhat unclear conditions.[4] They draft journalists who make a "Critic Rating" and non-journalists who make a "Public Rating". The ratings are gamified through a leaderboard "determined by the credibility and quantity of reviewed articles". The ratings themselves are either "Gold Cheese" or "Moldy Cheese" for articles and outlets of high or poor credibility.

These rating services are efforts to make it easier for the public to assess the trustworthiness of various outlets, but they also ironically make the news functionally less transparent. It becomes easy for the public to evaluate the transparency score, but rather opaque to assess the actual transparency. If news is already second-order information about the world, then ratings of that news is third-order information, pushing the public yet another step away from directly accessed information (Etzioni, 2010). Members of the public are not asked to evaluate and trust the news intermediary, but to evaluate and trust the ranking intermediary between the public and the news intermediary. Regardless of how many inter- mediaries are making checks on each other, the public must take a leap of faith and trust some of them in the absence of evidence.

While the additional transparency actors are not necessarily making the news more transparent to the public themselves, they are establishing an accountability system that is becoming increasingly recognized by various stakeholders. Since rationalized formal structures are sources of legitimacy, increased resource allocation, and survivability in *themselves* (Meyer & Rowan, 1977) *regardless* of the efficacy of transparency, then there are good reasons to keep them. Meyer and Rowan (1977, p. 345) hold that "As rationalized institutional rules arise in given domains of work activity, formal organizations form and expand by incorporating these rules as structural elements". The surfacing of organizations such as *Newsroom Transparency Tracker* and *Newsguard*, exemplified in Chapter 3, is built around the idea of transparency. Through their pre- sence and work towards applying transparency standards to news plat- forms around the world they are creating a centre of gravity to which news media must relate (e.g. Do we care about transparency? Are we transparent? Is this transparency?). This, then, is a confirmation of how the transparency myth of society at large is moving towards the inner core of the journalistic institution. The larger societal focus on trans- parency, the increased salience of transparency by high-status insiders, and transparency advocating and auditing standalone organizations together form an environment where the idea of transparency and what it can accomplish is repeatedly reinforced.

Meyer and Rowan (1977, p. 354) further suggest that "Institutionalized myths differ in the completeness with which they describe cause and effect relationships, and in the clarity with which they describe standards that should be used to evaluate outputs". Revisiting the claims made by esteemed actors in the field, the way in which causality will work is clear, as illustrated by the implicit theory of transparency. It is also evident that considerably less effort has gone into elaborating proper expressions of transparency and evaluating the actual output. More energy has been allocated for celebrating the myth than measuring its concrete effects (Meyer & Rowan, 1977). It offers a resounding yes to the general idea of "explaining how journalism is being made!" but is noticeably vague about the details of the inner workings of the journalistic news-creating processes that should specifically be explained to a layperson: how, by who, to whom, where, when, and with what expected effect. This is also visible in the lack of research into transparency policies; that is, research which investigates the script guiding transparency performances. It is easy to see the parallels to Fenster's (2006, p. 893) observation on transparency in government: "We have achieved rhetorical consensus regarding transparency's value and have generated costly and elaborate bureaucratic solutions in an effort to pursue it. But we have not actually achieved the goals of transparency in practice". In relation to journalism, I think that there are overlaps in rhetorical consensus and not achieving the goals in practice, but that we are not quite there yet in terms of elaborate bureaucratic solutions, and probably never will be, since journalism is driven by a different institutional logic than government.

In sum, the move towards transparency is subsequently, if my take on institutional theory has any bearing, more driven by the isomorphism of journalistic institutions with a larger societal trend than it is a decision by an autonomous institution trying to address a trust problem with its key constituents. Otherwise, I think we would see the opposite scenario, with efficient trust-creating actions and less in the way of theorizing and celebration.

This is not to say that proponents of transparency are ignorant or cynical; it is evident that their conviction is honest, and their arguments delivered in good faith. This is also not to say that transparency is unimportant, or that the public cannot be socialized into it; nor that the journalistic institution should not welcome transparency, as it clearly should, tactically, since embracing institutional myths increases legitimacy, resource allocation, and long-term survivability. But adhering to transparency is unlikely to solve journalism's current trust issues with the public, because the evidence so far supports neither the idea that the lack of transparency explains the decline in trust, nor that transparency is an efficient remedy.

In this context, it is worth reiterating from Chapter 4 that the reason the public identified algorithms as more credible was because they deemed them more *objective* – not more *transparent*. Some studies (Karlsson & Clerwall, 2019; Tandoc & Thomas, 2017, further detailed in Chapter 3) report that the public appreciates objectivity. Consequently, the problem might be how journalism delivers its objectivity promise, rather than the objectivity norm itself. At the same time, other studies have found transparency to have a positive effect (Curry & Stroud, 2019). These uncertain and somewhat contradicting results call for further scrutiny to tease out the aspects of objectivity and transparency – and the overlaps between them – that contribute to how journalistic trust varies among different segments of the public.

What is left of transparency?

This chapter has raised some critical and fundamental questions about the role of transparency in journalism, and what it is unable to do: it has also offered an explanation for its wholesale adoption by the institution in the absence of convincing evidence. If transparency is not *the*, or even *a* solution, what is the point of pushing for it even further? Despite the objections in this chapter there is also evidence that transparency has a role to play on some occasions, and there are also theoretical reasons to think it can be applied on other occasions. In the next chapter I will propose a few paths forward for journalism practice and studies. In my view it is important to stress these so that the applicable aspects of transparency are not lost, should transparency fall to the curse of high expectations.

Notes

1 Or any other "good" concepts, such as autonomy, independence, truth, objectivity, verification, citizens, and democracy, to mention a few that are frequently wielded in journalism.
2 Admittedly, it will be very difficult to draw straight lines from a decrease in funding in other parts of the organization to the cost of transparency measures, and further to the financial and legitimacy performance of the institution. Nevertheless, a similar calculation is at the heart of the implicit theory of transparency. Do A, and B is to follow.
3 Journalism is a semi-profession and it is difficult to make claims for exclusive professional knowledge, and thus a core; however, journalists still make decisions in their line of work that require discretion, and they often self-apply the term "professional" e.g. Society of Professional Journalists.
4 https://credder.com/ Website visited 3 March 2021. From the website it is evident that people can support them through Patreon. Their partner program "includes many free benefits" indicating that not all benefits are free and there is a fee involved, but details are available upon request.

References

Alt, J. E., Lassen, D. D., & Skilling, D. (2002). Fiscal transparency, gubernatorial approval, and the scale of government: Evidence from the states. *State Politics and Policy Quarterly*, 2(3), 230–250.

Ball, C. (2009). What is transparency? *Public Integrity*, 11(4), 293–308. https://doi.org/10.2753/PIN1099-9922110400.

Carlson, M. (2016). Metajournalistic discourse and the meanings of journalism: Definitional control, boundary work, and legitimation. *Communication Theory*, 26(4), 349–368. https://doi.org/10.1111/comt.12088.

Christensen, L. T., & Cornelissen, J. (2015). Organizational transparency as myth and metaphor. *European Journal of Social Theory*, 18(2), 132–149. https://doi.org/10.1177/1368431014555256.

Curry, A. L., & Stroud, N. J. (2019). The effects of journalistic transparency on credibility assessments and engagement intentions. *Journalism*. https://doi.org/10.1177/1464884919850387.

Curtin, D., & Meijer, A. J. (2006). Does transparency strengthen legitimacy? A critical analysis of European Union policy documents. *Information Polity*, 11(2), 109–122.

DiMaggio, P. J., & Powell, W. W. (1983). The iron cage revisited: Institutional isomorphism and collective rationality in organizational fields. *American Sociological Review*, 48(2), 147–160.

Etzioni, A. (2010). Is transparency the best disinfectant? *Journal of Political Philosophy*, 18(4), 389–404. https://doi.org/10.1111/j.1467-9760.2010.00366.x.

Fenster, M. (2006). The opacity of transparency. *Iowa Law Review*, 91(3), 885–949.

Fenster, M. (2015). Transparency in search of a theory. *European Journal of Social Theory*, 18(2), 150–167. https://doi.org/10.1177/1368431014555257.

Flyverbom, M. (2016). Transparency: Mediation and the management of visibilities. *International Journal of Communication*, 10(1), 110–122.

Fredriksson, M., & Edwards, L. (2019). Communicating under the regimes of divergent ideas: How public agencies in Sweden manage tensions between transparency and consistency. *Management Communication Quarterly*, 33(4), 548–580. https://doi.org/10.1177/0893318919859478.

Fung, A., Graham, M., & Weil, D. (2007). *Full Disclosure: The Perils and Promise of Transparency*. Cambridge University Press. https://doi.org/10.1111/j.1747-1346.2008.00128.x.

Gieryn, T. (1983). Boundary-work and the demarcation of science from non-science: Strains and interests in professional ideologies of scientists. *American Sociological Review*, 48(6), 781–795.

Grimmelikhuijsen, S. (2012). Linking transparency, knowledge and citizen trust in government: An experiment. *International Review of Administrative Sciences*, 78(1), 50–73. https://doi.org/10.1177/0020852311429667.

Hall, M. A., Dugan, E., Zheng, B., & Mishra, A. K. (2001). Trust in physicians and medical institutions: What is it, can it be measured, and does it matter? *Milbank Quarterly*, 79(4), 613–639. https://doi.org/10.1111/1468-0009.00223.

Han, B.-C. (2015). *The Transparency Society*. Stanford University Press.

Heim, K., & Craft, S. (2020). Transparency in journalism: Meanings, merits, and risks. In L. Wilkins & C. Christians (Eds.), *The Routledge Handbook of Mass Media Ethics* (pp. 308–320). Routledge.

Karlsson, M. (2010). Rituals of transparency: Evaluating online news outlets' uses of transparency rituals in the United States, United Kingdom and Sweden. *Journalism Studies*, 11(4), 535–545.

Karlsson, M. (2011). The immediacy of online news, the visibility of journalistic processes and a restructuring of journalistic authority. *Journalism*, 12(3), 279–295. https://doi.org/10.1177/1464884910388223.

Karlsson, M. (2020). Dispersing the opacity of transparency in journalism on the appeal of different forms of transparency to the general public. *Journalism Studies*, 21(3), 1795–1814. https://doi.org/10.1080/1461670X.2020.1790028.

Karlsson, M., & Clerwall, C. (2019). Cornerstones in journalism: According to citizens. *Journalism Studies*, 20(8), 1184–1199. https://doi.org/10.1080/1461670X.2018.1499436.

Karlsson, M., Clerwall, C., & Nord, L. (2017). Do not stand corrected: Transparency and users' attitudes to inaccurate news and corrections in online journalism. *Journalism & Mass Communication Quarterly*, 94(1), 148–167.

Kohring, M., & Matthes, J. (2007). Trust in news media: Development and validation of a multidimensional scale. *Communication Research*, 34(2), 231–252. https://doi.org/10.1177/0093650206298071.

Levay, C., & Waks, C. (2009). Professions and the pursuit of transparency in healthcare: Two cases of soft autonomy. *Organization Studies*, 30(5), 509–527. https://doi.org/10.1177/0170840609104396.

Lewis, J. D., & Weigert, A. (1985). Trust as a social reality. *Social Forces*, 63(4), 967–985. https://doi.org/10.1093/sf/63.4.967.

Lewis, S. C. (2012). The tension between professional control and open participation: Journalism and its boundaries. *Information, Communication & Society*, 15(6), 836–866. https://doi.org/10.1080/1369118X.2012.674150.

Mayer, R. C., Davis, J. H., & Schoorman, D. F. (1995). An integrative model of organizational trust. *The Academy of Management Review*, 20(3), 709–734.

Meyer, J. W., & Rowan, B. (1977). Institutionalized organizations: Formal structure as myth and ceremony. *American Journal of Sociology*, 83(2), 340–363.

O'Neill, O. (2002). *A Question of Trust: The BBC Reith Lectures 2002.* Cambridge University Press.

Örnebring, H., & Karlsson, M. (forthcoming). *Journalistic Autonomy: A Genealogy of a Concept.*

Plaisance, P. L. (2007). Transparency: An assessment of the Kantian roots of a key element in media ethics practice. *Journal of Mass Media Ethics*, 22(2–3), 187–207. https://doi.org/10.1080/08900520701315855.

Revers, M. (2014). The Twitterization of news making: Transparency and journalistic professionalism. *Journal of Communication*, 64(5), 806–826. https://doi.org/10.1111/jcom.12111.

Rourke, F. E. (1957). Secrecy in American bureaucracy. *Political Science Quarterly*, 72(4), 540–564.

Schoorman, F. D., Mayer, R. C., & Davis, J. H. (2007). An integrative model of organizational trust: Past, present, and future. *Academy of Management Review*, 32(2), 344–354.

Sennett, R. (2003). *Respect: The Formation of Character in an Age of Inequality.* Penguin Books.

Tandoc, E. C., & Thomas, R. J. (2017). Readers value objectivity over transparency. *Newspaper Research Journal,* 38(1), 32–45. https://doi.org/10.1177/0739532917698446.

Tuchman, G. (1972). Objectivity as a strategic ritual. *The American Journal of Sociology,* 77(4), 660–679.

Vos, T. (2020). Journalism as institution. In H. Örnebring (Ed.), *The Oxford Encyclopedia of Journalism Studies* (pp. 736–750). Oxford University Press.

Vos, T. P., & Craft, S. (2017). The discursive construction of journalistic transparency. *Journalism Studies,* 18(12), 1505–1522. https://doi.org/10.1080/1461670X.2015.1135754.

6 Transparency after all?

Caleb woke up on the morning of Wednesday 3 September 1957, took his newspaper from the mailbox, and noticed that there was a smudge on the front page of his beloved local paper, the *Rocky Mountain News*. Eager to know how this came about, he hurried inside the house to phone the print shop. He got hold of the chief printer and asked what happened. "Well", said the printer, happy about the interest in how his machinery worked, "We had a bit of a problem with the printing press tonight and the team had to make good use of their spanners to take care of the problem". "Oh, deary me, how intriguing", said Caleb, before wanting to know more about the brand of the spanners used. Were they from *Britool*, perhaps the "Superslim" line from *Williams*, or, in Caleb's view, king of the hill, German brand *Gedore*?

As absurd as this example is, we are happily ready to accept the basic premise behind it when welcoming transparency; that is, the idea that detailed knowledge of journalism is a top priority for the public,[1] that people have a large appetite for and sufficient expertise to understand how journalism works, and that they are delighted to spend the resources necessary to seek this knowledge out, be it how algorithms are programmed, how errors are corrected, the political leanings of a journalist, or, from the mock example above, why the aesthetics of a printed paper failed. Closely related to this idea is the idea that people's views of journalism are mostly based on journalistic performance. This might certainly be true for some people, but for most it is probably not. Chapter 3 showed that changing journalistic performance (e.g. making it more transparent) did not do much to move people's perceptions in any direction. Chapter 5 went head-on with the rhetoric of transparency through some theoretical interventions. Other questions arise from the ridiculous example above, and the empirical evidence presented earlier. If not all forms of transparency performance provide the predicted outcome, when and where is what kind of transparency needed for whom, to explain or justify what, to what kind of public?

DOI: 10.4324/9780429340642-6

Having focused on the failure to deliver according to the hype and the limits of transparency thus far, this sixth chapter ends the book on a slightly more positive note, and provides suggestions about how transparency can still play a role in journalism, even if that role might be different and perhaps smaller than currently hoped for. Transparency might play a larger role in times of crisis, or when different parts of the public (e.g. high vs low trust and consumption) demand different kinds of transparency for different kinds of reasons. The chapter will end by suggesting a future research agenda detailing a number of potential studies that hopefully can better inform researchers, practitioners, students, and the public about what transparency can and cannot do.

Before looking into future research, I offer a retrospective on the waves of transparency's role in journalism so far.

Three waves of transparency in journalism

Based on my findings in the previous chapters, as well as observations from my own experience of studying the phenomenon in journalism practice and consulting the research in the area, I have identified three "waves" in the discussion about transparency in journalism. There is a first *foundational* wave, followed by a second wave of *consolidation*, and a third and ongoing wave which is marked by both *hope* and *scrutiny*. Although each wave has a character of its own, there are also overlaps. For instance, in the first wave, the discussion centred around what transparency was and what it could do. This was not absent from later stages of the discussion, but the overall focus became much more empirical and practical. Until recently journalism practice has also mostly guided the research agenda, and it is not meaningful to separate the two.

The first wave of interest in journalistic transparency took off in the first few years of the 2000s, as detailed in Chapter 1. This wave was primarily concerned with translating the general notion of transparency into journalism; in other words, coming to terms with what transparency, this thing talked about in other institutional contexts, was, what it is supposed to do, and how it could possibly be adapted to and benefit journalism. The outcome of this work was what I labelled earlier in the book the implicit theory of transparency, which served as a stepping stone for later research, and hence, the univocal yet somewhat astonishing findings in recent experimental studies that there is literally no transparency effect. At this stage, there were few research projects looking into the area and they were similarly trying to understand the concept of transparency, to determine how it could be applied in journalism and what possible frictions could arise.

The second wave is discernible in the period somewhere around 2010–2016. In this wave there were more explicit formulations of the implicit transparency theory, and a consolidation of what transparency is, trying to pin down how the abstract concept of transparency is put to work when practiced in journalism. There was also some theorizing about the triangulation of transparency, journalism and the character-istics of digital media and emerging platforms, especially Twitter (Karlsson, 2011; Lasorsa, 2012; Lasorsa et al., 2012; Revers, 2014). Relatedly, there was also increased empirical attention directed at the way mostly journalists, but also the public, viewed transparency. At around this time, transparency started making its way into the core of journalism as it was taken up as an articulate norm in codes of ethics, and, thus, became institutionalized. This wave also included examples of larger empirical research projects being launched in the area, most of them showing a limited return from transparency.

The third wave, arguably from 2016 and continuing today, consists of two parallel parts, *hope* and *scrutiny.* Hope can be attributed to trans-parency as a readily available tool (through the inclusion of transparency by SPJ in 2014 and RTDNA in 2015) to help address and counter the decline/questioning of established social institutions, as forcefully illu-strated by the 2016 events of Brexit and the election of Donald Trump as the president of the US. Parallel to this *hope* strand, there was also an intensified systematic empirical *scrutiny* of transparency from researchers, as reported in Chapter 3. In addition to the areas that were scrutinized pre-2016 (e.g. journalists, content, the public) the research interest also expanded into algorithms and platforms, and the challenges they pose to transparency (as illustrated in Chapter 4).

Several of the studies referred to in this book were published just months before the book was finished, so there is probably a backlog of studies waiting to be published. The overall impression from these studies is, expressed broadly, that transparency does not matter a great deal to the public. Through these diverging trends – hope in the public debate and scrutiny-turned-rude-awakening by many research projects – a more autonomous research agenda is notable.

I think we face even more difficult challenges dealing with the issues raised in Chapter 4 regarding the role of algorithms in journalism and their transparency. In addition, it is now time to assess the limitations and variations of transparency in different settings (e.g. countries, genres, situations, publics), as most research so far has been relatively limited in scope compared to other ambitious comparative projects in journalism studies (Hanitzsch et al., 2011; Mellado et al., 2017; Weaver & Willnat, 2012). The remainder of the chapter will suggest a few pertinent research areas. Before proposing specific research topics, I will make use of the concepts of "transparency pathways" (Fox, 2007) and "targeted transparency" (Fung et al., 2007) to recommend a general approach to researching transparency in journalism. These concepts can help move the transparency discussion even further from rhetorical consensus to efficacy, a move that is necessary regardless of how big, small, or non-existent the return.

Transparency pathways

Regardless of the kinds of institutions that consider, are encouraged, or are intimidated into adopting transparency, they are faced with finding a general approach and way of working that can translate into daily performance. Fox (2007, p. 665) discusses two different "transparency pathways", through which institutions can relate to transparency: "Instruments for public access to information generally fall into one of two categories: proactive and demand-driven". The proactive approach is information dissemination on behalf of the institution, and the demand-driven approach is when an institution's public, for a range of reasons, request information and explanations from an institution that are not readily available.

Different approaches are helpful in unpacking a key problem in the current debate on journalistic transparency. The demand-driven pathway to transparency is the one that has been touted so far in the rhetoric: the public expects transparency and when the demand has been saturated increased levels of trust are to follow. Actual institutional behaviour, however, has been about disseminating information from their own needs, such as asking what they want to do to be transparent, and how the public should react to that. A gap between transparency-in-rhetoric and transparency-in-practice makes it problematic to measure the efficacy of transparency.

The dissemination approach is not flawed by default, but it does not sound out the public's demand for transparency systematically, and thus leaves meeting this demand to pure chance. It would be perfectly fine to decide on a simple dissemination approach, but this cannot be followed by trustworthy claims of meeting demand. It is also misguided at best and dishonest at worst to advertise a dissemination approach as a demand approach, because it conceals where the true mandate is from. If it is not the public who put transparency in motion, it must be other actors who gave it a push, whether deliberate or unintentional, and those dynamics should be pursued by research. If research is encapsulated by demand-driven rhetoric, however, the proper questions will not be asked.

The proactive dissemination approach could also be a way to both socialize the public into a transparency norm, and to use transparency to anticipate and counteract critique which would only show in the longer term. While the outcomes of the two approaches might be alike in so far as the same information might be publicly available in the end, their underlying logics are different. The dissemination approach is more guided by institutional need, and the demand-driven approach by the needs of (segments of) the public, and this should not be confused. A key issue for any researcher would be the extent to which the transparency measures taken respond to the different logics.

The transparency research so far has departed from an everyday scenario where journalism is publishing news that people may or may not read without being overly engaged with either the news story or the journalistic outlet. Evidently, that does not make a great deal of a difference to the public, if the results of experimental studies have any bearing. There is another dimension of demand-driven transparency that is not currently considered in the literature – the need for transparency in journalism during non-normal or crisis situations. From crisis communication research we know that the interest in a topic and in the behaviour of involved parties skyrockets when something is called into question. It would be interesting to determine whether transparency is more called for in a crisis, and if this has a greater impact on the trustworthiness of journalism. This is true both for a crisis in other social institutions (e.g. government), and for the journalistic institution (e.g. when it is called into question). It can be theoretically proposed, following the increased need for information in times of crisis, that transparency is more sought after in a crisis and that, tentatively, a track record of transparent behaviour is rewarded.

Targeted transparency

One of the transparency pathways is driven by demand from the public. Journalism studies and research do not have a great track record of investigating the kind of transparency, if any, that the public wants (but see Chapter 3 for some exceptions). Luckily, there are cues from research in other areas regarding what might work. Fung et al. (2007) suggest what they refer to as "targeted transparency" to understand when and why transparency measures work. Targeted transparency is the connection between information and action; that is, that a certain kind of information will be followed by a related action or outcome. In order for that to happen both the information and action needs to be defined. In journalism, this could be articulated in the idea that disclosing how the news material was gathered (information) leads to members of the public reading this additional information (action), resulting in a changed or reinforced perception of the news story, journalists, or news outlet (outcome). Formulating various transparency measures in this way also allows the rate of success to be considered at each step, and the whole process to be evaluated. This can be formulated as a set of questions: Where were the news gathering processes explained and published? Was this additional information read? Did this change the evaluation of the news story, its author, or the outlet? These three simple questions could obviously be supplemented with other more complex questions, but they indicate the general issue to be addressed: What is transparency more specifically, and what is the expected and actual outcome of its use?

An emphasis on the link between information and action means that targeted transparency is a concept that enables a vital step toward the efficacy of transparency and away from the rhetorical consensus about the transparency myth (as discussed in Chapter 5, but see also Christensen & Cornelissen, 2015; Fenster, 2006; Meyer & Rowan, 1977). Fung et al. (2007) propose that there are two success factors for targeted transparency. The first success factor is that measures are user-centred. By this they mean (p. xiv):

> Targeted transparency policies were effective only when they provided facts that people wanted in times, places, and ways that enabled them to act. That is, effective polices were those that succeeded in embedding new information in users and disclosers existing decision-making routines. That meant that the starting point for any transparent policy was an understanding of the priorities and capacities of diverse audiences who might use the new information.

The most successful transparency measures in journalism would thus be to add information to known bottlenecks and areas of contention in journalism (e.g. to what extent a journalist's personal preferences affect their output, that there is an inevitable gatekeeping process at work etc.). There is little knowledge about how those areas of concern overlap between journalists and the public, since, as repeatedly pointed out in the book, the view from the public is rarely considered, and especially not through more open-ended methodologies that seek to understand public preferences on their terms, rather than how they react to issues which are interesting to journalists. Those views might also not be valued, understood, or distributed evenly in a population. This can be compared to the current situation where journalistic transparency is largely modelled after what journalism considers it needs (Heim & Craft, 2020).

The second success factor is that user-centred measures need to be sustainable. This means that the measures must be in place for a while, and need to be adapted, because they are rarely perfect in their first instance. People must have the opportunity to become accustomed to them, determine how they work, and provide feedback. In line with this view, any transparency feature that is in place for a longer period is thus more likely to be successful. This is something that research needs to be better at evaluating, since most, if not all, previous research is cross-sectional. The time dimension of sustainability is yet to be decided, but it took decades for objectivity to become widely accepted, from its first formal inception in the 1920s.

In any case, taking the public's views into account is crucial if transparency is to have any chance of creating better relationships between journalism and the public. Otherwise, transparency risks being reduced to an obsessive audit of quantifiable micro-level actions that have no other outcome than draining journalism of resources better used elsewhere (see Christensen & Cheney, 2015, for an extended argument in this spirit).

Suggestions for a future research agenda

Theoretically, transparency is expected to work in a certain way, but in practice the story is rather different. What journalistic transparency is, and the role it is supposed to serve, has thus so far been understood as defined by strong institutional insiders (i.e. professional organizations and industry leaders). If transparency is to be something more than just a strategic management of visibility, the public should have a greater say about it. A first step in this direction would be to bring in new perspectives, and the concepts of a transparency pathway and targeted transparency offer new approaches to journalistic transparency. This includes, as mentioned before, unpacking the actors (beyond the public) who are advocating transparency, and have power over how transparency should be defined, redefined, understood, implemented, and justified.

In the next sections I propose a research agenda and make some detailed suggestions for future research that lean on the concepts of transparency pathways and targeted transparency. The recommended future strands of research are structured along the different components of the participatory transparency model. Departing from the idea that transparency needs to demonstrate efficacy for its long-term sustainability, the appraisal will start with effects and go backwards from there.

Effects

There are several areas of effect that are uncharted. First, there is a need to investigate more thoroughly the *conversion* appeal of transparency. The conversion argument lies implicitly in the role that transparency serves as a trust-gaining tool, but the extent to which it sways people who are suspicious of journalism is, if not doubtful, at least unknown. A broader question to ask, putting transparency into context, is under what conditions will a person sceptical of journalism become more positive, and what role, if any, does transparency play in that process?

Another issue is the *socialization* effect of transparency. It may very well turn out in the future that transparency will have a positive impact on trust. One version of this is that transparency, according to the implicit theory of transparency, has worked and the public's need for transparency has been met. Another version is that citizens have been educated to appreciate transparency, rather than that their sovereign demands have been met. Theoretically, this is an important distinction, as in the latter case *any* norm can hypothetically be pushed and accepted as good journalism, as long as it is used sufficiently and coherently. Let us not forget that the core argument of the implicit transparency theory is that transparency is supposed to be a measure that the public demand to make up for opaque/bad journalistic practice. If there is no or little demand from the public, then transparency cannot be a strong explanatory factor for either an increase or decrease in trust. This can be investigated empirically by asking whether an increased use of transparency is to be followed by its increased appreciation. The sustainable dimension of targeted transparency described by Fung et al. (2007) suggests this is so, but it is also a question of whether transparency will have a better, worse, or similar socialization effect in comparison with competing norms (i.e. objectivity).

Thirdly, would the public want more transparency if journalism was more embedded in another institutional logic? In Chapter 2 I argued that there are different dynamics at play in government and journalism, as you can walk away from the latter but not from the former (see also O'Neill, 2002). We also noted in Chapter 3 that the public at best have lukewarm feelings regarding transparency. Maybe these two matters are connected. Translated into an empirical question: Would people demand more transparency from journalism if they were *forced* to consume it or deal with its consequences? Or, less dramatically, do the demand, desire, and appreciation of various expressions of transparency correlate with the perceived intrusion of journalism into one's life, or on matters that are important to someone? Another issue related to the interrelationship with different institutions involves whether the demand, desire, and appreciation for transparency in journalism correlate with journalism's perceived autonomy from governmental and other institutions.

The fourth and final suggestion for effect research is that it is time to bring in more context. We need to know more about how universal the effects, or lack thereof, of transparency are. What happens to an effect if various contexts are considered, for instance cultural/social contexts (between countries, geographical areas within countries)? What socio-psychological factors among the public (social interactions, worldviews, attitudes, habits) are transparency effects contingent upon? Will the status of the journalist play a role (will a star reporter need less transparency or be more rewarded for transparency than a newcomer to the field)? How is organizational affiliation involved (different kinds of news providers, professionals and others, mainstream and alternative)? Will it work similarly for the institution at large, the profession, and the individual media worker? Studies following this line of enquiry would add to our knowledge of transparency, as the typical study so far is only concerned with transparency in one place and one point in time.

Actors

In general, we know far too little about the public (or rather publics, in the plural) who, while not often present on the stage, still play an important role. Currently, the public's view of transparency is either imagined or considered from the perspective of how the journalistic institution wishes them to react. One problem, paraphrasing Fenster (2006, p. 928, see also Fung et al., 2007), is that there is an assumption that there is an existing audience out there which needs and wants to be fully informed about the inner workings of journalism. If people can have a rational ignorance about politics (Curtin & Meijer, 2006; Fenster, 2006), which arguably affects them more tangibly than journalism, then rational ignorance about journalism would probably be even greater. Departing from that notion, we should ask under what circumstances it would be rational for the public to pay close attention to how journalism works.

There are also several other questions that the public should be asked. One is what information the public is concerned about regarding journalism. Seeing information is not enough, however, as knowledge involves additional processes, including systematic cognitive bias (Ananny & Crawford, 2018; Etzioni, 2010). The public should therefore also be queried about their ability and motivation to decode information about transparency in journalism; that is, how do people understand information about journalism, and how do they act on that information under different circumstances?

Another question involves the relative importance of transparency. Since everything in journalism consumes resources, the role of transparency should be considered in relation to other aspects of journalism. Would the public prefer transparent journalism if this was offset by fewer news stories? Or, would they welcome more transparent journalism if they had to pay more for it?

Most members of the public would probably agree that it is neither possible nor preferable for journalism to be open about everything. In addition to asking them what kind of openness they desire (if any), it could also be interesting to consider their ideas of appropriate un-open journalism. Since, as argued in Chapter 5, there will always be a backstage area in journalism, it would be pertinent to ask the public what part of journalistic work, and under what circumstances, would they trust journalists to employ their own discretion.

The above questions about the public could also be focused specifically on how they understand and appreciate the role of algorithms in journalism (as detailed in Chapter 4). In particular, it would be interesting to further investigate the conditions under which algorithms are more trusted than journalists. Further, it would be fascinating to learn how the public relates to the problem of the Russian doll, detailed in Chapter 4 – that is, the many layers of external actors who are involved in shaping the way news stories are gathered, selected, processed, published, and distributed. To what extent are they satisfied with a scenario where it is not clear who is responsible for, or at least could answer questions about, the content published on a news website?

The standalone auxiliary actors who promote and audit transparency, exemplified in this book by the *Newsroom Transparency Tracker* and *Newsguard*, should receive more attention. In terms of performance metaphors, they could be seen as *critics* who are not visible on the stage or heard by the public, but whose presence is felt in the minds of the actors performing on stage. As with all critiques, some will be more important than others. We need to better understand how they contribute to the discourse about transparency. What are the institutional overlaps between these actors and other actors within and outside the journalistic institution? How do they understand and define transparency, and how consistent are those definitions with other definitions? What are their roles in terms of information brokers in various networks? What leverage do they have over journalism?

The organizations (e.g. software producers, data miners, large social media platforms) that provide the algorithms and the data that shape journalistic work and output are another set of actors. It would be enlightening to identify their standards and views of transparency, and the extent to which they overlap with those of journalism. It would also be interesting to see who will have to cave in when different principles clash. Relatedly, this raises the question of how far backstage the public can walk before the final curtain comes down.

The actors we probably know most about from previous research are the journalists themselves, but more could be done here too. In addition to the comparative approaches mentioned earlier, longitudinal studies would be welcome. This would allow us to see whether the official sanction of the norm has affected the outlook of journalists and the extent to which this affects newcomers and incumbents in the field differently. Further studies examining what good transparency practices mean to them and their relationship with the public could also be illuminating. Since journalists are most closely affected, and even replaced, by algorithms it would be interesting to see how they relate to the Russian doll issue highlighted in Chapter 4, because when algorithms enter the newsroom, journalists are for once on the short end of information asymmetry in journalistic news production. It would be interesting to compare their views of information asymmetry to those of the public, and to see whether views about the lack of transparency are universal. To reiterate the question posed in relation to the public: To what extent are journalists satisfied with a scenario where it is not clear who is responsible for, or at least could answer questions about, the content published on a news website?

Script

The script is there to provide guidance on how transparency should be performed, and this needs more consideration: how the acceptance of transparency at the institutional level (i.e. by professional organizations and industry leaders) is interpreted and appropriated (or not) by the various journalistic outlets in the field. The line of inquiry could follow, but not be limited to, several questions. For instance, to what extent has the general notion of transparency been translated into scripts guiding daily work, what is expressed in them, and do the scripts differ between context and outlets? How detailed are they regarding the definition of what transparency is and what it should accomplish? When, where, and by who should transparency be delivered? Are there different scripts for different genres (e.g. sport vs politics)? How are the scripts negotiated in daily practice, and by whom? Are there, to extend the performance metaphor, *prompters* who support, guide, and monitor journalistic behaviour in the newsroom?

Aesthetics and delivery

There are quite elaborate understandings of what transparency is predicted to accomplish (trust), and the means of doing so (e.g. admitting and correcting errors, explaining framing etc.). If transparency does have a strong performative component, it is strange that the forms of those performances are rarely studied, if at all. To address this, there is need for research that explores the aesthetics of transparency in terms of language, signs, symbols, and design elements. More specifically, it could be asked, for instance, if transparency measures should be published together with or in the vicinity of news content, and where this is positioned (e.g. at the top, on the side, or below the news story)? We know little of the modes of delivery that are used – text, photos, videos, graphics, badges, boxes, and so on. This lack of attention to the form of news is not limited to transparency, as extraordinarily little attention is paid to the visual and design aspects of journalism overall (Barnhurst & Nerone, 2001). Research into the form of transparency could thus also help develop this area generally, in journalism studies.

Similarly, little is known about how transparency messages are composed, if they differ in tonality and affect compared to regular journalism, and if that would matter. This line of research could be concerned with how transparency techniques are expressed currently, but could also explore fitting and more efficient ways to implement it in the future. Other aesthetic and delivery issues involve how the public would like to be able to communicate with journalists. In the example mentioned in Chapter 4, there was no transparency pathway into the *Star Tribune* other than a generic "corrections" e-mail address. There was even less contact information for the Associated Press, not to mention determining the actors involved in any particular news story in Automated Insights and Zacks Investment Research. An empirical question could ask what an appropriate and cost-efficient way of communicating "Matters concerning transparency over here" would be.

Stage

The stage is the place where transparency is enacted. There has been disproportionate attention directed towards Twitter in previous research, in relation to its marginal role for the general public. If we consider the idea that the key actors are involved in defining transparency, who it is for, and what stage it should perform on, then the prominence of Twitter is telling. Evidently, this is the main stage for the key public – that is, peers and elites. Elites are also invested in the transparency myth, again indicating a need to study how and by whom journalistic transparency is discursively constructed.

Since the performance changes with the stage, other stages need attention too, especially those where the public is located. Currently that means social network services such as Facebook and Instagram but that might be subject to change. There is still ample need for research into the main platforms of journalism – websites and apps. Although much of the transparency debate has been intertwined with digital media, there are other forms of transparency too. For instance, the ombudsman as a focus for transparency, or other analogous initiatives such as town-hall-type meetings and other gatherings, where journalists and members of the public meet face-to-face. These kinds of activities might very well offer more in terms of efficacy than technology-oriented solutions, but unless we make the comparisons we will not know.

Not so disruptive after all

This book has attempted to clarify, illustrate, and critique the role of transparency in journalism. Hopefully, it has provided some answers and raised even more questions, but most of the work remains to be done. Great work lies ahead in building an empirically grounded and developed theory of transparency in journalism. Theoretically, transparency is believed to change journalism greatly, including how it is performed and how the public views it. In that sense, the implementation of transparency can be viewed as a disruption; however, in practice that has not been the case so far. Rather than a grand explosion it has been a splutter, as the public has not been compelled to take a leap of faith. Transparency is still something of a conundrum in need of solving.

A key issue is the power to define what journalistic transparency is: how we have come to accept transparency the way we have and what alternative views have been overlooked. In particular this includes more in-depth knowledge of the benefactors of journalistic transparency, if it is not the public. Transparency is often seen as an accountability instrument, but a less explored path is how transparency measures, or the lack thereof, are being evaluated in terms of accountability. What are considered appropriate enforceable punishments when applicable measures and levels of transparency are not met, and who is to enforce the punishments? Because if journalism alone sets the standards, evaluates whether standards have been met, and hands out punishments if standards are breached, we have returned to information asymmetry and trusting/not trusting journalism to handle its own issues.

Moving the discussion forward, then, we should consider different points of departure than the implicit theory of transparency. The philosopher Onora O'Neill makes the case that at some point trust must be placed without guarantees. The key issue, then, for the trustor, is to place trust with *care* (O'Neill, 2002). Focusing on the dimensions of the trustor's care, and the conditions under which the trustor cares, will lead to a rather different set of questions. For instance, instead of asking "In what ways should journalism be open?" it would be more productive to start with "What leaps of faith are the public willing to make?" and "What would journalism have to do for the public to take that leap?" These questions should in particular be posed to the media-sceptic public, as it is they who have to make the biggest leap, and arguably, have the largest complaints about journalism.

Still, what the public want is one thing, and what journalism wants is not necessarily the same. Obviously, journalism relies on the public for revenue and legitimacy, but it cannot fully submit to the public since that would be to give up its autonomy. A good start would be determining whether there is any common ground, and what that consists of. What, to paraphrase Fenster (2006, p. 885), are the mutually acceptable levels of journalistic transparency *and* opacity, if any?

Note

1 I disregard the fact that there is no "one public" for reasons of convenience. What appeals to different publics will most likely vary.

References

Ananny, M., & Crawford, K. (2018). Seeing without knowing: Limitations of the transparency ideal and its application to algorithmic accountability. *New Media and Society*, 20(3), 973–989. https://doi.org/10.1177/1461444816676645.

Barnhurst, K. G., & Nerone, J. C. (2001). *The Form of News*. The Guilford Press.

Christensen, L. T., & Cheney, G. (2015). Peering into transparency: Challenging ideals, proxies, and organizational practices. *Communication Theory*, 25(1), 70–90. https://doi.org/10.1111/comt.12052.

Christensen, L. T., & Cornelissen, J. (2015). Organizational transparency as myth and metaphor. *European Journal of Social Theory*, 18(2), 132–149. https://doi.org/10.1177/1368431014555256.

Curtin, D., & Meijer, A. J. (2006). Does transparency strengthen legitimacy? *Information Polity*, 11(2), 109–122.

Etzioni, A. (2010). Is transparency the best disinfectant? *Journal of Political Philosophy*, 18(4), 389–404. https://doi.org/10.1111/j.1467-9760.2010.00366.x.

Fenster, M. (2006). The opacity of transparency. *Iowa Law Review*, 91(3), 885–949.

Fox, J. (2007). The uncertain relationship between transparency and accountability. *Development in Practice*, 17(4–5), 663–671. https://doi.org/10.1080/09614520701469955.

Fung, A., Graham, M., & Weil, D. (2007). *Full Disclosure: The Perils and Promise of Transparency*. Cambridge University Press. https://doi.org/10.1111/j.1747-1346.2008.00128.x.

Hanitzsch, T., Hanusch, F., Mellado, C., Anikina, M., Berganza, R., Cangoz, I., Coman, M., Hamada, B., Elena Hernández, M., Karadjov, C. D., Virginia Moreira, S., Mwesige, P. G., Plaisance, P. L., Reich, Z., Seethaler, J., Skewes, E. A., Vardiansyah Noor, D., & Kee Wang Yuen, E. (2011). Mapping journalism cultures across nations. *Journalism Studies*, 12(3), 273–293. https://doi.org/10.1080/1461670X.2010.512502.

Heim, K., & Craft, S. (2020). Transparency in journalism: Meanings, merits, and risks. In L. Wilkins & C. Christians (Eds.), *The Routledge Handbook of Mass Media Ethics* (pp. 308–320). Routledge.

Karlsson, M. (2011). The immediacy of online news, the visibility of journalistic processes and a restructuring of journalistic authority. *Journalism*, 12(3), 279–295. https://doi.org/10.1177/1464884910388223.

Lasorsa, D. (2012). Transparency and other journalistic norms on Twitter. *Journalism Studies*, 13(2), 402–417. https://doi.org/10.1080/1461670X.2012.657909.

Lasorsa, D. L., Lewis, S. C., & Holton, A. E. (2012). Normalizing Twitter journalism practice in an emerging communication space. *Journalism Studies*, 13(4), 19–36.

Mellado, C., Hellmueller, L., Márquez-Ramírez, M., Humanes, M. L., Sparks, C., Stepinska, A., Pasti, S., Schielicke, A.-M., Tandoc, E., & Wang, H. (2017). The hybridization of journalistic cultures: A comparative study of journalistic role performance. *Journal of Communication*, 67(6), 944–967. https://doi.org/10.1111/jcom.12339.

Meyer, J. W., & Rowan, B. (1977). Institutionalized organizations: Formal structure as myth and ceremony. *American Journal of Sociology*, 83(2), 340–363.

O'Neill, O. (2002). *A Question of Trust: The BBC Reith Lectures 2002*. Cambridge University Press.

Revers, M. (2014). The Twitterization of news making: Transparency and journalistic professionalism. *Journal of Communication*, 64(5), 806–826. https://doi.org/10.1111/jcom.12111.

Weaver, D., & Willnat, L. (2012). Journalists in the 21st century. In D. Weaver & L. Willnat (Eds.), *The Global Journalist in the 21st Century* (pp. 529–551). Routledge.

Index

Page numbers in **bold** indicate information in tables. Those followed by 'n' indicate notes.